The Filipino Instant Pot Cookbook For Beginners

100 Tasty Filipino Instant Pot Electric Pressure Cooker Recipes for Beginners and Food Lovers

(2nd Edition Revised)

Melanie Diwata

Copyright © 2020

All rights reserved. Except as permitted under the U.S. Copyright Act of 1976, the scanning, uploading and distribution of this book via the Internet or via any other means without the express permission of the author is illegal and punishable by law. Please purchase only authorized electronic editions, and do not participate in or encourage electronic piracy of copyrighted material.

All rights reserved.

Contents

Introduction 1

The Beginner's Guide to Multicookers 2

    Why is there so much crave for Multicookers? 2

    Multicookers and Safety 3

    The Multicooker Basic Button Functions 3

    The Fancy button Functions 5

    Other fancy buttons functions you can use 5

    How to Keep your Multicooker Clean 6

Breakfast 9

    Chicken Rice 9

    Filipino Leche Puto (Steamed Cake with Flan) 11

    Coconut Tapioca with Fruit 13

    Champorado Chocolate Rice Pudding 15

    Chicken Potatoes Smoor 16

    Nasi Pandan Wangi 18

    Young Jackfruit Curry Sayur Nangka 19

    Coconut Mango Sticky Rice 21

    Rice Pudding 22

    Puto Maya Rice Cakes 23

    Boiled Peanuts Nilagang Mani 24

    Guisado Mung Beans with Chicharon 25

    Achari Aloo Baingan 26

    Rice Beans 28

    Sweet Punjabi Lassi 29

    Filipino Mousse 30

    Black Forest Bread Pudding 31

    Turnip Cake 32

    Tofu Pudding 34

Lunch 36

    Beef Nilaga Filipino Beef and Vegetable Soup 36

    Filipino Style Spaghetti 37

    Mie Sop Ayam Medan 38

    Filipino Chicken Soup 40

    Pancit 41

    Orange Chicken Lettuce Wraps 42

    Filipino Edamame Spaghetti Squash 44

    Lechon Asad 46

    Smoked Salmon Chowder 47

    Fish Chowder 49

    Fish Biryani 51

    Chicken Macaroni Soup 53

    Chicken and Dumplings 54

    Noodle Bowls 56

    Jambalaya Soup 57

    Clam Chowder 59

    Garlic Noodles 60

    Corn on the Cob 61

    Fish Stew 62

    Easy Filipino Fried Rice 63

    Steamed Crab Legs 65

    Shrimp Fried Rice 66

    Pork Shoulder Soup 68

    Kabocha Squash Rice 70

    Filipino Green Beans 71

Dinner 72

    Filipino Style Picadillo 72

    Mung Bean Stew 74

    Mechado Beef Stew with Coconut Milk and Salted Peanuts 75

Filipino-Style Chicken Curry	77
Panang Curry	79
Massaman	80
Filipino Pork Chops Steak	82
Chicken Afritada	83
Ginger Soy Chicken	85
Sticky Ribs	86
Filipino-Style Pork Belly	88
Filipino Spaghetti Sauce	89
Chicken Paws	90
Chicken with Paprika and Butternut Squash	92
Beef Potato Curry	93
Kaffir Chicken	95
Soy Sauce Braised Pork	96
Lu Rou Fan	97
Arroz Caldo with Chicken	98
Chicken Adobo and Gravy	99
Filipino Steak Chops	100
Creamy Lemon Garlic Chicken	101
Ilonggo Pork Spare	103
Garlic Beef	104
Monggo Curry	105
Paksiw Na Lechon	106
Filipino Pork Pata Tim	107
Cashew Adobo Chicken	108
Coconut Pork	109
Filipino Inspired Steamed Ginger Scallion Fish	111
Honey Garlic Shrimp	113
Mechado Filipino Beef Stew	114
Soy Sauce Chicken Rice	116
Pinoy Whole Chicken	117

Taiwan Inspired Filipino Braised Pork 118
Orange Chicken 120
Sweet Sour Chicken 122
Filipino Asian Pork Shoulder 123

Introduction

Multicookers and pressure cookers are one of the most popular kitchen appliances that can make your life easier and the cooking process more fun! Various dishes can be cooked with the Multicooker and it can also save you time as the process of cooking is really simple. It is important to remember the basic tips of how to use the Multicooker if you want it to last long for you:

1. Carefully read the manual for the device. It will save you from unpleasant surprises when it comes to cooking.
2. Do not overfill the cooker. Always know the maximum content limit for the version of your Multicooker.
3. Always add liquid. You should always have at least some liquid in the pot.
4. Release the pressure right. Always follow the recipe details on how to release the pressure.

With Multicookers, it will be no brainer for you to cook delicious and exotic Filipino recipes. Filipino cuisines are developed from different cultures and it is very varied. It has traces from Spanish and Mexican cuisines, though it resembles other Southern Asian cuisines a lot.

Filipino cuisine is probably the least spicy of all South Asian countries. But do not think that it doesn't have vivid taste, it does. Instead of spices, Filipino cuisine presupposes using lots of herbs, garlic, onions and ginger to add flavor to the dishes. That helps to preserve the vivid taste of the food itself, not covering it with the spices.

On average, Filipinos eat four meals a day: breakfast, lunch, dinner and afternoon snack. For breakfast people have coffee, fried rice, eggs or salted bread buns. Lunch and Dinner doesn't have any particular food, they can include any Filipino dishes.

The most popular Filipino dishes are rice and rice cakes, noodles, ulam (pork, chicken, and beef, in different variations), different salads.

In this book you will find different Filipino recipes, the ones that are traditional and can be found only in the Philippines, and also the ones that can be found in other parts of Asia but are also a part of Filipino cuisines. With the help of a Multicooker, you will be able to cook these dishes quickly and without spending too much time on the cooking process.

The Beginner's Guide to Multicookers

A multicooker is an electronically controlled multi-cooking device that is designed to help users prepare tasty, delicious meals using pressure and slow cooking techniques. Its history dates back to the 1920s in the United kindom. Ever since then, many other multi-cooker models, with amazing functionalities, have been introduced and have grown become a main-stay in most homes in North America and the world at large.

Why is there so much crave for Multicookers?

The answer is pretty simple. The mad rush for multi-cookers is simply due to the cutting edge technology behind it. Imagine cutting your regular cooking time in half or by as much as 60%, you know what that means when you have hungry kids preparing to go to school early in the morning. Or you have a hungry spouse that needs to be in the office as early as 7 am, you can't afford to waste time preparing their meals so they don't get late to work and earn a query from their boss.

Multicookers and pressure cookers let you cook extremely fast using its pressure cooking functionality, or slow cook, using its slow cooking feature. Another important reason why many people love Multicookers is that they can program the device to cook, while they attend to other important activities. The programmable features of

Multicookers are very helpful for busy people who need to multi-task as well as attend other important activities.

Multicookers and Safety

Multicookers are one of the safest kitchen electric gadgets you can find in the world due to the safety features as well as the electronically programmable functions they come packed with. You can't go wrong when using Multicookers with regards to safety, as there are several safety features all acting as redundancies to each other.

One of the most notable safety features of a Multicooker is the two safety catches attached to the lid. One of which acts as a lock mechanism that prevents the opening of the Multicooker when it's in operation, and the other acts as an automatic excess pressure release mechanism. If for any reason the pressure release mechanism fails to function as designed, an extra layer of safety feature activates and shuts off the heating element, especially when an excess build of pressure has been detected.

Despite the safety features included in our Multicookers, we should also ensure we read our user manuals thoroughly to ensure that our Multicookers are used safely. One of the important safety requirements by most multicooker and pressure cooker manuals is to ensure that the valve steam release is free from obstruction of any sort. Remember that the valve release is designed to allow excess pressure to escape from your multicooker or pressure cooker. Obstruction of the valve release will trap excess pressure in the Multicooker which could cause serious burns or injury if the hot content spills on you.

The Multicooker Basic Button Functions

Before I delve into the specific function buttons, let's get familiar with the frequently used buttons otherwise known as the main buttons. The main buttons on the Multicooker you'll be using most of the time include "Saute," "Manual," "Pressure," "Adjust," and "+" and "–".

- **Manual:** The manual button is one of the most frequently used buttons on the Multicooker and can be used to cook most food as well as save for fermented glutinous rice or yogurt. To use the manual button when you want to start the cooking process, you'll need to place your food securely in the Multicooker and seal, with the pressure release switched to sealing. Now press the manual button once, and then use the "+" and "– " button to set the appropriate time you want, and then you can go and attend to other important activities. In the meantime, Your Multicooker will function as programed and would stop when it reaches the set completion time.

    By default, most Multicookers are set to high, with a pressure that ranges from 10.2 – 11.6 psi and a temperature of 239°F. Depending on what you are cooking, you can lower the pressure and temperature to around 5.5 – 7.2 psi and 229 – 233°F respectively.

- **Sauté:** The Saute button is perfect for keeping your meat in top condition ready to be pressurized. Without the Saute button, meat can appear pale and stale. But if you want to make your meat appear, toasty, roasty before pressure cooking, then the Saute button will come in handy. The Saute functionality operates within 3 temperature ranges: "Normal" (320 – 349 °F), "more" (347 - 410°F) and "less" (275 -302 °F). You can toggle between these temperature ranges by using the "Adjust" button.

  Apart from Sauteing and searing, the Saute button can be used to thicken and simmer sauces after cooking. However, you'll need to keep an eye on while simmering the sauces by stirring frequently because the bottom of your Multicooker can get too hot.

- **Keep Warm/Cancel:** If you want to stop the pressure cooking process, then the Cancel button is pretty much the right button for you. This functionality is really important especially if you need to dash off somewhere or you forgot to add a few spices and ingredients to your meal. A single press of the keep warm/cancel button puts the Multicooker on standby mode, but then if it's depressed again, the Multicooker goes into the Warm mode. Note! Some Multicooker models have these botton functions separated.

  The temperature range of the warm mode hovers within 145 - 172°F, however, you don't have to press the Keep Warm button at the end of the normal cooking process. Most Multicookers are designed to automatically engage the Keep warm functionality at the end of the cooking program you choose. It can stay in the keep warm mode for up to 99 hours and 50 minutes.

- **Pressure:** The pressure functionality is pretty much straight forward from its name. You can use the pressure button to change the pressure of almost all Multicooker settings except Saute, yogurt and slow cook.

- **+ and - :** This button is mainly used to change the cooking times of the manual cooking function. However, the button doesn't work if you use any of the preprogrammed button functions.

- **Adjust:** The adjust button is mainly used to make changes to cooking times of preprogrammed buttons such as beans. However, you won't be able to do that with rice in certain brands. You can also use it to choose a yogurt program if you want.

The Fancy button Functions

The fancy button functions involve those buttons that have been preprogrammed to cook popular, common foods in a certain way. According to the makers of some Multicookers, there are technology-based smart microchips built-in to control the way popular foods are prepared by combining four parameters efficiently. These four parameters include temperature, heating intensity, pressure, and duration.

- **Beans/Chili Function:** This cooking functionality comes with a very strong start when engaged and it does that by ramping up both pressure and temperature quickly. It's programmed to last for 39-minutes and can hold both pressure and temperature at 11 psi and 230°F respectively.

- **Soup Function:** The soup button functionality is pretty much straightforward. It is used to make broth, soup or stock. When operating using this mode, the Multicooker will maintain or control a particular temperature and pressure so that your soup or stock doesn't heavily boil. You can choose to adjust the cooking time to whatever you want, usually between 20-40 minutes. You can also adjust the pressure to either high or low.

- **Multigrain function:** The multigrain function is mainly used for cooking several grain foods. It starts its operation at 140 degrees, 50-minute soak to soften things up, and then it raises the temperature to 248°F and pressure to a little less than 11psi, which it then maintains for nine more minutes.

- **Meat/stew Function:** This button is mainly used for meat and stew preparation. The program duration is designed to last for 28-minutes, and the temperature hovers around 230 °F and pressure within the range of 8.7 psi, which is higher than the manual "low" setting but low by normal operating standards.

- **Congee Function:** This functionality shares a lot of similarities with the "meat/stew" function. The temperature setting for the congee function hovers around 230°F, while its pressure hangs around 8 psi.

Notwithstanding, most of the button functions mentioned above can be manipulated in more recent multicookers by pressing their respective buttons. You can change their operation from "Normal" to "More" or "Less." When you use the "More" setting, you can expect the food to be cooked a lot faster, while the "Less" setting will cook the food a lot slower.

Other fancy buttons functions you can use

Most of the pre-programmed buttons have pressure cooking capabilities; however, there are a few buttons that don't possess pressure cooking capabilities. They include "slow cook," "Saute," and "yogurt." The Saute button functionality has already been discussed above. Now let's look at the other two.

Slow Cook: The Slow Cook button is meant for meals that require the lower cooking temperature to cook efficiently. There are three modes in the Slow Cook functionality. They include "Normal" which operates within the temperature range of 190 – 200° F, while the "Less" temperature setting falls within 180 – 190°F, and "More" 200 - 210°F. Other brands of slow cookers may have different temperature parameters. But then, it won't be far off from what was stated above.

Yogurt: This button lets you prepare your favorite yogurt drink with ease. You only need about 8 cups of whole milk and 1/4 cup of plain whole milk yogurt (Note, you'll need to ensure your yogurt milk is plain with active and live cultures else your yogurt preparation won't work). Pour 7 cups milk into the inner pot of your Multicooker, and then close it.

Next, set the pressure release valve to venting. Now, it's time to press the Yogurt button until your Multicooker's display shows boil. Your Multicooker will heat the milk within an hour. When done, the Multicooker will make a beep and then stop heating, and then the display will show Yogurt. Now it's time to cool the milk to 105 - 115°F (you can monitor the temperature using a digital thermometer). You can let the milk sit on a counter to cool naturally or you can place the inner pot in a bowl of ice water to speed things up.

Next, remove the skin of the milk that appears at the top of the heated milk. This will ensure your yogurt gets a creamier appearance and taste. Next, Get a medium bowl and then pour the last cup of milk along with the milk yogurt into it and then stir properly.

Next, add the mixed content to the inner pot containing the cooled milk with temperature ranging between 105 - 115°F. Now, return the inner pot to the Multicooker, Press the Yogurt button and then set timer automatically to 8 hours. When done, transfer the content to storage containers and then refrigerate. Serve chilled and enjoy. This right here is the hidden bonus recipe for everyone.

How to Keep your Multicooker Clean

The Multicooker is a versatile piece of cooking gadget that can be found in most homes around the world. Due to its versatility, efficiency and reliability, it's subjected to extensive use by most users. Keeping the Multicooker clean can become difficult for most people. Different types of ingredients and foods are cooked in a Multicooker, with some of the leftovers being extremely difficult to get rid of. There two types of cleaning methods you can use to maintain the appearance of your Multicooker, one of which is the Everyday Cleaning Method and the other is the Deep Cleaning Method.

Everyday cleaning method and tips (After each use)

- **Wash the inner pot:** The beauty of most Multicookers is the fact that most of their components are dishwasher safe. First of all, unplug the Multicooker, and then you can put the inner pot in a dishwasher, and watch it do its thing.
- **Wipe it down:** Once the dishwasher has done its job, use a very clean cloth to gently wipe it down on both the inside and outside of your Multicooker.
- **Wipe the inside of the lid:** The lid of most pots is one part that is easily forgotten during the cleaning process, especially the inside part of the lid. Unfortunately, it's one of the dirtiest parts of the Multicooker owing to the job it performs.
- **Clean the sealing ring:** After each use, you should endeavor to clean the silicone ring that's located on the inside of the lid. If you fail to clean the sealing ring regularly, it will absorb food odors and colors.

Deep Cleaning Process and Tips (Every few weeks)

The everyday cleaning process and tips are quite good for maintaining the appearance of your Multicooker. However, there are stubborn to reach places as well as dirt that are almost impossible to remove using regular everyday cleaning tips or techniques. Follow these steps when you want to deep clean your Multicooker.

Step 1 – Unplug

To avoid potential electric shocks, it's advisable to unplug your Multicooker each time you are about to clean it up.

Step 2 – Clean up the Housing Unit

Use a slightly damp, clean rag to wipe both the inside and outside of your Multicooker "housing unit." Next, using a small brush, scrub and remove any residue that must have been left at the bottom of the pot after the cooking process. Ensure you reach the nooks and crannies using the brush.

Step 3 – Wash the lid

Using your hand and a soft sponge, wash the lid of your Multicooker. This should be the easiest part of the deep cleaning process.

Step 4 – Inspect the smaller parts for stains

The smaller parts and components of your Multicooker can easily be clogged by food, dirt, and stains. Ensure you thoroughly inspect them and then clean them out if you find dirt. Remove the quick release handle by pulling it with a little pressure. Wash it with soap water thoroughly and return it to its position.

Next, check the inside of the lid; you should see a shield that covers the steam valve. Remove it, and then wash and replace it. Inspect the condensation cup that is attached to your Multicooker, if you see any dirt, do the needful and then return it to its location.

Step 5 – Clean the sealing ring

Try to inspect the sealing ring that is located under the lid. First of all, check for damage. If any damage is detected, replace the sealing ring as fast as possible. These parts are commonly available in most stores online. If the sealing ring isn't damaged, check for dirt. If dirty, hand wash or wash at the top rack of your dishwasher. Once you are done with the cleaning or washing process of the sealing ring, return it to its position and ensure it's seated in the correct position.

Step 6 – Wash the accessories and inner pot

Also ensure that the accessories of your Multicooker, such as steam rack, are thoroughly washed. The steam rack and inner pot are quite sturdy and dishwasher safe. So you can use your dishwasher to wash these parts regularly. Check your user manual to see other accessories that you can use with the dishwasher. Once you are done washing the inner pot, use a paper towel to wipe it clean.

You can add some vinegar to the paper towel if you detect the presence of detergent residue. Vinegar removes these residues and keeps your Multicooker inner finishing shiny. Do not be tempted to use steel sponges or brushes on the finishing to avoid scratches and damages.

Step 7 – Time to reassemble

Once you are done with the cleaning process, it's time to reassemble your Multicooker component so you can return it to doing what it does best. Be careful not to forget the smaller parts such as valve shield, sealing ring, and the quick-release handle when reassembling.

Now that we are done with the introductory part of this book, it's time to delve into the world of delicious Filipino recipes and delicacies. Go through the recipes, prepare them and enjoy with your friends and families.

Breakfast

Chicken Rice

Cooking Time: 30 minutes

Servings: 4

Ingredients

- 1 cup uncooked jasmine rice, rinsed and drained
- 4 boneless skinless chicken thighs
- 1 cup chicken broth
- 2 carrots, chopped
- 1 bell pepper, chopped
- ½ onion, chopped
- 3 cloves garlic, minced
- 1 tablespoon peanut oil
- 2 teaspoons ginger, minced
- 2 teaspoons cumin powder
- 1 tablespoon soy sauce
- 1 teaspoon sesame oil and toasted sesame seeds
- Salt and pepper, to taste

Instructions

1. Add the chicken to a bowl and season it with salt and pepper. Set aside to marinate.
2. Press sauté function on the Multicooker and add peanut oil for 5 minutes until it shows hot. Add onions and cook for 3 minutes.
3. Add garlic, ginger and cumin. Cook for 3 minutes then turn off sauté mode.
4. Add chicken broth and scrape the bottom. Add carrots and pepper.
5. Add the rice to the Multicooker and top with chicken thighs.
6. Drizzle with soy sauce and do not mix. Close the lid and position the vent to sealing. Set to manual mode for about 10 minutes.

7. When done naturally release pressure for 8 minutes. Quick release and shred the chicken.
8. Sprinkle with sesame oil and seeds and mix well. Serve and enjoy!

Nutritional info (Per serving): 417 calories; 10.9 g fat; 46 g total carbs; 32 g protein

Filipino Leche Puto (Steamed Cake with Flan)

Cooking Time: 25 minutes

Servings: 4

Ingredients

Flan:

- 2 egg yolks
- ½ can condensed milk
- ½ tablespoon lemon extract

Puto (Steamed cake):

- ¼ cup unsalted butter, room temperature
- 2 egg whites
- ½ cup sugar
- 1 cup cake flour
- ¼ cup milk
- 2 teaspoons baking powder
- 2 cups warm water for steaming
- melted butter for brushing the mold

Instructions

1. Mix the eggs, condensed milk and lemon extract in a medium bowl. Set aside.
2. Combine butter egg whites, sugar, cake flour, baking powder and milk in another bowl. Set aside.
3. Add 2 cup of warm water into the pot and set it to steam function. Place a metallic trivet inside and then add a steamer.
4. Grease the molds with melted butter; pour 1/3 of flan into each mold. Place into the Multicooker.
5. Steam for 5 minutes then pour the mixture on top and continue to steam for 15 minutes. Remove from the pot.
6. Let it cool and serve. Enjoy!

Nutritional info (per serving): 175 calories; 166.5 g fat; 70 g total carbs; 11 g protein

Coconut Tapioca with Fruit

Cooking Time: 30 minutes

Servings: 8

Ingredients

- 1 cup small tapioca pearls
- 6 cups water
- 1 cup sugar
- 1 13.5 oz. can coconut milk
- 1 30 oz. can fruit cocktail in heavy syrup, undrained
- 1 bottle nata de coco, undrained
- 1 15 oz. can mandarin oranges, drained
- 1 can Shirakiku Mixed Fruit with nata de coco, undrained
- 1 can Lychee quartered, undrained
- 1 tablespoon vanilla extract
- Salt, to taste

Instructions

1. Place a small pot over medium high heat, add 6 cups of water and bring the water to a boil. Set the hot water aside
2. Preheat the Multicooker for a few minutes then press the sauté mode. Add hot water and turn off the cooker.
3. Add tapioca and mix well, seal the Multicooker, press manual and cook for 3 minutes in high pressure.
4. Naturally release pressure for 10 minutes. Open the lid, stir and pour the mixture to a bowl. Cover with foil and set aside for 10 minutes.
5. Add sugar and salt. Stir and let it cool. Add coconut milk, vanilla mixed fruit, Lychee, mandarin oranges, nata de coco and fruit cocktail and mix well. Place in the refrigerator to cool.
6. Serve and enjoy!

Nutritional info (Per serving): 168 calories; 11 g fat; 15 g total carbs; 22 g protein

Champorado Chocolate Rice Pudding

Cooking Time: 15 minutes

Servings: 2

Ingredients

- 1 cup sweet short grain rice, rinsed and drained
- 2 cups coconut milk, unsweetened
- 1 cup malted cocoa powder
- 1 cup coconut sugar
- 1 cup heavy cream
- ½ cup dark chocolate chips
- 1 teaspoon Himalayan Sea salt

Instructions

1. Add the rice into the Multicooker and add water.
2. Press "Rice" button and set for 8 minutes. When done natural release the pressure.
3. Open the Multicooker, press "Sauté" function.
4. Add cocoa powder, coconut milk, sea salt and chocolate chips. Stir well until the chips are dissolved.
5. Add coconut sugar. Serve drizzled with heavy cream on top.
6. Enjoy while hot!

Nutritional info (per serving): 171 calories; 5 g fat; 4 g total carbs; 24 g protein

Chicken Potatoes Smoor

Cooking Time: 40 minutes

Servings: 4

Ingredients

- 35.3 oz. bone-in drumsticks You can use other cut of chicken
- 600 gr potatoes peeled and cut into 2-inch pieces
- 2 tablespoons cooking oil
- ¼ cup Water
- 8 shallots
- 5 cloves garlic
- 1-inch fresh ginger

Spices:

- ½ teaspoon nutmeg powder
- 1 teaspoon coriander powder
- 3 bay leaves

Seasoning:

- 4 tablespoons kecap manis
- 1 tablespoon soy sauce
- ¼ teaspoon ground white pepper
- 2 tablespoons brown sugar
- 1 teaspoon sugar
- Salt, to taste

Instructions

1. Add the shallots, ginger and garlic to a food processor and grind them finely. Set aside.
2. Press the Sauté button on the multicooker and add oil, preheat the Multicooker. Add the ground shallots mixture and cook for 3 minutes.
3. Add the chicken and cook, including spices and bay leaves. Finally add the seasoning ingredients and ¼ cup of water. Press cancel

4. Press high pressure and cook for 18 minutes. Naturally release pressure and remove the chicken, set aside.
5. Press sauté function and add the potatoes. Cook for 10 minutes until tender.
6. Serve and enjoy while hot!

Nutritional info (per serving): 324 calories; 5 g fat; 75 g total carbs; 7.2 g protein

Nasi Pandan Wangi

Cooking Time: 20 minutes

Servings: 4

Ingredients

- 2 cups white long-grain rice, well rinsed
- 1 cup water
- 1 cup pandan juice
- ½ cup coconut milk
- Salt, to taste

Instructions

1. Add all the ingredients to the Multicooker and stir well to combine.
2. Close the lid and press the Rice button. Set the timer to 5 minutes.
3. Quick release the pressure, add coconut oil if you want and serve.

Nutritional info (per serving): 58 calories; 1 g fat; 10 g total carbs; 3 g protein

Young Jackfruit Curry Sayur Nangka

Cooking Time: 30 minutes

Servings: 8

Ingredients

- 17.5 oz. young jackfruit, rinsed and drained
- 9 oz. green beans, chopped
- 7 oz. canned red beans, rinsed and drained
- 3 tablespoons cooking oil
- 4 cups water
- 2 cups coconut milk
- 8 shallots peeled
- 5 garlic peeled
- 5 Thai chili
- 10 cayenne chili pepper
- 3 Fresno chili pepper
- 1 inch fresh ginger

Spices:

- 2 teaspoon galangal powder
- 1 tablespoon turmeric powder
- 1 cinnamon stick
- 1 tablespoon coriander powder
- 4 cardamom pods
- 4 cloves

Herbs and seasonings:

- 5 bay leaves
- 5 kaffir lime leaves
- 1 cube of chicken bouillon
- Salt
- 4 tablespoons coconut sugar

Instructions

1. Add the shallots, garlic, thai chili, ginger, cayenne and fresno chili to the food processor and grind until fine. Set aside.
2. Press the Sauté button on the Multicooker and add oil. When hot add spices and herbs and cook for about 5 minutes.
3. Add jackfruit, green beans, red beans, water, chicken bouillon, chili mixture and stir to combine.
4. Cover, turn the valve to seal, press "Pressure cook", high pressure and set the timer to 15 minutes. When done wait for 5 minutes to release pressure.
5. Add coconut milk, salt, sugar and seasoning. Serve and enjoy!

Nutritional info (per serving): 168 calories; 13 g fat; 12.7 g total carbs; 4.3 g protein

Coconut Mango Sticky Rice

Cooking Time: 30 minutes

Servings: 2

Ingredients

- 1 cup glutinous rice, rinsed and drained
- 3 ¼ cups water
- 1 cup canned coconut milk
- ¼ cup sugar
- 1 ripe mango, peeled and cubed
- 1 pandan leaf knotted
- 1 tablespoon black sesame seeds
- Salt, to taste

Instructions

1. Pour 2 cups of water into the Multicooker. Place the trivet on top.
2. Add the rice to a stainless steel bowl, add 1 ¼ cup water and place on the trivet. Close the lid, turn the steam handle to sealing, press "Pressure cook", high pressure and set timer to 15 minutes
3. Place a skillet over medium heat add 1 cup of coconut milk, sugar, salt and pandan leaves. Let it simmer as the sugar dissolves. Take out the leaves.
4. When rice is done, wait for 10 minutes to release pressure, turn the steam valve to venting and remove the lid carefully.
5. Remove rice from the Multicooker and pour half of the coconut mixture to the rice, cover and let it sit for a minute.
6. Serve rice with sauce, cubed mangoes and sesame seeds. Enjoy!

Nutritional info (per serving): 180 calories; 16 g fat; 3.5 g total carbs; 9.7 g protein

Rice Pudding

Cooking Time: 40 minutes

Servings: 4

Ingredients

- 1 cup long-grain rice, rinsed and drained
- 2 cups 2% milk
- 1 ½ cups water
- 8 oz sweetened condensed milk
- ¾ cup raisins
- 1 teaspoon vanilla extract
- 1 teaspoon ground cinnamon
- Salt, to taste

Instructions

1. Add the rice to the Multicooker.
2. Add milk, vanilla extract, cinnamon and salt. Stir. Close the lid, press "Porridge" function and set the timer to 20 minutes.
3. Release the pressure naturally for about 10 minutes. Do a quick release for about 5 minutes and carefully remove the lid.
4. Add condensed milk and raisins. Stir and serve immediately. Enjoy the rice pudding!

Nutritional info (Per serving): 332 calories; 5.2 g fat; 63.8 g total carbs; 8.4 g protein

Puto Maya Rice Cakes

Cooking Time: 20 minutes + freezing time

Servings: 4

Ingredients

- 1 ½ cups glutinous white rice
- 3 cups water
- 3 cups coconut cream (canned)
- ½ cup granulated sugar
- 1 cup coconut meat slivers, grated
- 1 cup mangoes, cubed
- ½ teaspoon finely minced fresh ginger
- 12 pieces banana leaves, washed well

Instructions

1. Add the rice to a large bowl and add water to soak. Refrigerate for about 8-10 hours, drain rice and set aside.
2. In the Multicooker combine rice, coconut cream, sugar, ginger and salt. Close the lid and set the valve to sealing position, press "Rice" and cook on low pressure for 12 minutes.
3. When done and the timer goes off, do a quick release, unlock the pot and transfer rice to a greased cake pan.
4. Fill the Multicooker with 4 cups of water, put a metallic trivet inside and place the cake pan on the trivet. Close the lid, set the valve to sealing, press high pressure, steam for 5 minutes. When done and the timer goes off do a quick release. Open lid.
5. Scoop the rice and shape into mounds, place on the banana leaves. Serve with cubed mangoes and coconut meat slivers. Enjoy!

Nutritional info (Per serving): 97 calories; 8 g fat; 25 g total carbs; 11 g protein

Boiled Peanuts Nilagang Mani

Cooking Time: 1 hour 20 minutes

Servings: 4

Ingredients

- 4 cups raw peanuts with shell, washed thoroughly
- 10 cups water
- ¼ cup salt

Instructions

1. Add the peanuts to the Multicooker, add water and salt.
2. Put a heavy pan on the peanuts to prevent them from floating
3. Close the lid tightly, press Manual, high pressure and set the timer to 1 hour 20 minutes. Do a quick release.
4. Drain excess water and cool the peanuts. Serve and enjoy!

Nutritional info (Per serving): 143 calories; 12 g fat; 14 g total carbs; 17 g protein

Guisado Mung Beans with Chicharon

Cooking Time: 50 minutes

Servings: 4

Ingredients

- 1 cup dried mung beans
- 2 cups water
- 2 Tablespoons vegetable oil
- 2 cloves garlic, minced
- 1 onion, chopped
- 1 tomato, chopped
- 1 Tablespoon fish sauce
- 2 cups cooked pork adobo pork belly, cubed
- 4 cups vegetable broth
- 1 cup chicharron (pork rinds)
- Salt and pepper, to taste

Instructions

1. Place the mung beans to a large bowl, add water and soak for about ½ an hour. Drain water and set aside the beans.
2. Press the Sauté function on the Multicooker and add oil.
3. Sauté the onions, garlic and tomatoes for 2 minutes. Add fish sauce and mix, click cancel to turn it off.
4. Add the beans, broth, cooked adobo cubes, salt and pepper. Close the lid, set the valve to sealing position. Press Manual, high pressure and cook for 15 minutes. Do a quick release when the timer goes off.
5. Serve and garnish with chicharron. Enjoy!

Nutritional info (Per serving): 64 calories; 7 g fat; 1 g total carbs; 1 g protein

Achari Aloo Baingan

Cooking Time: 15 minutes

Servings: 3

Ingredients

- 8 small eggplants
- 2 potatoes, chopped
- ½ cup water
- 2 tablespoons mustard oil
- 1 onion, diced
- 3 teaspoons garlic, minced
- 2 teaspoons ginger, minced

Spices

- 2 teaspoons dried mango powder (amchur)
- 2 teaspoons fennel powder
- 1 teaspoon coriander powder
- 1 teaspoon garam masala
- 1 teaspoon paprika
- 1 teaspoon roasted cumin powder*
- 1 teaspoon salt
- 1 teaspoon turmeric
- ½ teaspoon fenugreek seed powder
- ¼ teaspoon black pepper
- ¼ teaspoon carom seeds (ajwain)
- ¼ teaspoon nigella seeds (kalonji)
- ¼ teaspoon cayenne

Instructions

1. Add the eggplants to a shallow dish and use a knife to make deep slits. Add oil and let it get hot.
2. Add onions and cook for 7 minutes. Add garlic, ginger, spices and potatoes mix well.

3. Add eggplants and water. Close the lid tightly, set the valve to seal, press Manual and high pressure and set the timer to 4 minutes. Quick release the pressure.
4. Open the lid and remove from the Multicooker. Serve and enjoy!

Nutritional info (Per serving): 249 calories; 23 g fat; 7 g total carbs; 7 g protein

Rice Beans

Cooking Time: 30 minutes

Servings: 4

Ingredients:

- 1 ¼ cup dry red kidney beans
- 1 ½ cup dry brown rice
- 1 cup salsa
- ½ bunch cilantro, stems and leaves divided
- 3 cups vegetable broth
- 2 cups water

Instructions:

1. Add beans and rice to the Multicooker.
2. Add broth, water and stir.
3. Add salsa and cilantro stems.
4. Close the lid, set valve to Sealed, press Manual, and cook on High for 25 minutes. When done release pressure, press "Warm" button.
5. Move valve to Venting to release pressure.

Nutritional info (per serving): 175 calories; 166.5 g fat; 70 g total carbs; 11 g protein

Sweet Punjabi Lassi

Cooking Time: 15 minutes

Servings: 2

Ingredients:

- 2 cups plain yogurt
- ½ cup water
- 4 tablespoons sugar
- ¼ teaspoon green cardamom powder
- ½ teaspoon rose water

Instructions:

1. Combine water and yoghurt in a small bowl.
2. Pour this mixture to the Multicooker.
3. Add green cardamom powder and sugar. Close the lid, press Manual. Cook on High pressure for 10 minutes. Release the pressure.
4. Open the lid, add rose water before serving.

Nutritional info (per serving): 213 calories; 8 g fat; 28 g total carbs; 9 g protein

Filipino Mousse

Cooking Time: 15 minutes + freezing time

Servings: 4

Ingredients:

- 4 egg yolks
- ½ cup swerve
- ¼ cup water
- ½ cup cacao
- 1 cup whipping cream
- ½ cup almond milk
- ½ teaspoon vanilla
- salt

Instructions:

1. Whisk egg in a bowl. Set aside.
2. Add swerve, egg, water and cacao to a pan and mix well.
3. Add almond milk, cream and mix in the pan.
4. Let it sit for 5 minutes, and then add vanilla and salt.
5. Place the pan over medium low heat, gently add 1 tablespoon of warm chocolate.
6. Put this mixture in jars. Set aside.
7. Add 1 ½ cups of water to the Multicooker, place a metallic trivet on top.
8. Place jars on the trivet, close the lid, and set Manual at High pressure for 6 minutes. Quick release the pressure.
9. Open the lid and take out jars.
10. Refrigerate for 6 hours before serving.

Nutritional info (per serving): 110 calories; 8 g fat; 5 g total carbs; 3 g protein

Black Forest Bread Pudding

Cooking Time: 35 minutes

Servings: 6

Ingredients:

- 4 eggs
- 1 cup heavy cream, plus more for dribbling
- ⅓ cup packed dark brown sugar
- 9 cups cubed challah bread
- ½ cup frozen cherries
- 3 tablespoons cocoa powder
- ¼ teaspoon ground cinnamon
- confectioners' sugar for dusting
- salt

Instructions:

1. Prepare a round 7 cup heatproof container by greasing it softened butter.
2. Combine eggs, cream, sugar, cocoa powder, salt and cinnamon in a food processor. Pulse for ½ minute.
3. Place bread in a shallow bowl and add the egg mixture from the food processor.
4. Add cherries and mix well, then transfer batter to the greased dish. Set aside for 10 minutes while covered with foil.
5. To the Multicooker, add 1 ½ cups of water, place the metallic trivet, place the pan with pudding batter on top of the trivet.
6. Close the lid, set valve to Sealed, choose Manual and cook for 25 minutes. Let the pressure release naturally and open the lid.
7. Take out the bread pudding.
8. Dust with confectioners' sugar.

Nutritional info (per serving): 297 calories; 12.3 g fat; 39 g total carbs; 9 g protein

Turnip Cake

Cooking Time: 5 hours 30 minutes

Servings: 6

Ingredients:

- 1.45 lbs. turnip julienne
- 2 tablespoons peanut oil
- 2 teaspoons roasted sesame oil
- 2 sausages, chopped
- 2.5 tablespoons Chinese cured meat, chopped
- 3 tablespoons dried shrimp
- 3 pieces cooked dried scallops
- rice flour mixture
- 1/3 lbs. rice flour
- 2.5 tablespoons water chestnut flour
- 1 tablespoon sugar
- ½ teaspoon white pepper
- 1 cup chicken stock
- salt

Instructions:

1. To the Multicooker, add 1 cup of water and place a metal trivet.
2. Put a stainless steel bowl on the trivet and layer turnips. Close the lid, set valve to Sealed, pressure cook on High pressure for 10 minutes, then do a quick release. Open the lid.
3. Meanwhile, combine the rice flour mixture ingredients in a medium bowl and set aside.
4. When turnips are done, discard excess water.
5. Add sausages and cured meat to the Multicooker, press the Sauté mode, cook for 3 minutes.
6. Adds shrimp, peanut oil and sesame oil. Make sure to scrape the bottom.

7. Add 1/3 of the rice flour mixture and mix well. Pour this mixture into a cake pan.
8. Clean the Multicooker, add 1 cup water and place a trivet in the Multicooker. Place the cake pan on the trivet.
9. Close the lid, set valve to Sealed, pressure cook on High pressure for 32 minutes. Naturally release after 20 minutes and remove the lid.
10. Remove cake pan and set aside to cool in the fridge for 4 hours.

Nutritional info (per serving): 381 calories; 11.6 g fat; 28 g total carbs; 39 g protein

Tofu Pudding

Cooking Time: 30 minutes + Soaking time

Servings: 6

Ingredients:

- soy milk
- 1 cup dry soybeans
- 3 cups cold water for soaking
- 6 cups cold water
- a pinch of salt
- tofu pudding
- 1 teaspoon agar-agar powder
- 3 tablespoons granulated sugar
- ginger syrup
- 7 oz. rock sugar
- 3 tablespoons brown sugar
- 3 tablespoons ginger, crushed

Instructions:

1. Add soy beans and 3 cups water to a container and soak it for 12 hours in the refrigerator.
2. Blend soaked soy beans with 2 cups cold clean water until smooth.
3. Place a steamer basket in the Multicooker; add salt and 4 cups of water.
4. Add blended soy mixture. Close the lid, set valve to Sealed, cook on High pressure for 5 minutes. Natural release the pressure after 25 minutes and open the lid.
5. To a sauce pan add sugar, 1 cup water, brown sugar and crushed ginger. Bring it to a boil, lower the heat and let it simmer for 2 minutes.
6. Scoop crushed ginger and discard. Remove from the heat and let it cool.
7. Strain soy milk in a pan and add agar-agar powder.
8. Bring tofu pudding mixture to a boil to ensure agar-agar powder dissolves fully.
9. Add granulated sugar and let it simmer. Take off from the heat and let it cool at room temperature.

Nutritional info (per serving): 232 calories; 3.5 g fat; 47 g total carbs; 6 g protein

Lunch

Beef Nilaga Filipino Beef and Vegetable Soup

Cooking Time: 40 hour

Servings: 6

Ingredients

- 1 lb. beef neck bones
- 1 lb. beef stew meat, cubed
- 2 cups onions, chopped
- 2 tablespoons whole peppercorns
- 7 cups water
- ½ head of cabbage, thinly sliced
- 1 sweet potato, cubed
- 3 carrots, chopped
- Salt, to taste

Instructions

1. Add all the ingredients except the vegetables to the Multicooker.
2. Cover and cook on Manual for 30 minutes at 375F. Do the natural release.
3. Add the remaining ingredients and press Sauté button. Cook until potatoes are tender. Serve.

Nutritional info (Per serving): 168 calories; 11 g fat; 15 g total carbs; 22 g protein

Filipino Style Spaghetti

Cooking Time: 15 minutes

Servings: 4

Ingredients

- 1 lb. ground chicken
- 1 lb. Spaghetti Noodles, break in half
- 24 oz. Great Value Chunky Tomato, Garlic and Onion Pasta Sauce
- 9 oz. Jufran Banana Sauce
- 24 oz. water
- 1 shallot, minced
- 2 tablespoons vegetable oil
- 2 garlic cloves, minced

Instructions

1. Preheat the Multicooker on Sauté mode until it shows hot. Add vegetable oil.
2. Cook the shallots and garlic for about 4 minutes. Add chicken and sauté until it browns. Turn it off.
3. Place the spaghetti on top of the chicken.
4. Mix in the Jufran sauce, pasta sauce and water. Press the noodles down; do not mix to make sure it's slightly submerged in water.
5. Press Manual mode, high pressure and cook for 7 minutes. Quick release pressure and turn off the Multicooker.
6. Open the lid and stir well to mix. Serve and enjoy!

Nutritional info (per serving): 475 calories; 8 g fat; 89 g total carbs; 10 g protein

Mie Sop Ayam Medan

Cooking Time: 30 minutes

Servings: 8

Ingredients

- 1 lb. spaghetti noodles
- 1 lb. rice noodle stick
- 1 tablespoon cooking oil
- 3 lbs. bone-in skin-on chicken leg
- 1 cinnamon stick
- 2 stalks lemongrass trim off woody ends
- 5 stalks celery, leaves for garnish
- 8 cups water
- 1 block chicken bouillon
- Salt
- cooking oil for deep-frying

Spices and herbs:

- 3 cardamoms
- 6 bay leaves
- 5 cloves
- 1 star anise
- 1 tsp whole white peppercorns

Green Chili:

- 1.8 oz. green chili, destemed
- ¼ teaspoon salt

Instructions

1. Cook the noodles according to directions on the package, set aside

2. Place a small pot of water over medium heat and add green chili. Boil them until tender then use an immersion blender to blend them. Season with salt and set aside to chill in the refrigerator.
3. Preheat the Multicooker by pressing the sauté mode until it says "hot", add 1 tablespoon oil.
4. Cook the ground spices for about one minute. Ad cinnamon, lemongrass, chicken and water.
5. Add spices and herbs ingredients, close lid tightly, turn vent position to seal, press manual, high pressure and set to 20 minutes.
6. When the timer beeps wait release the pressure naturally. Open the lid and take out the chicken meat, set aside the soup.
7. Add oil for frying and heat it up. Fry the chicken meat until golden and crunchy. Remove from heat and shred the meat using two forks.
8. Serve equal portions of yellow noodles, rice stick noodles and shredded chicken meat.

Nutritional info (per serving): 475 calories; 8 g fat; 89 g total carbs; 10 g protein

Filipino Chicken Soup

Cooking Time: 40 minutes

Servings: 4

Ingredients

Chicken broth:

- 4 frozen bone-in skin-on chicken thighs
- 2 cups chicken stock
- 2 slices ginger
- 4 green onions, chopped

Soup ingredients:

- 4 carrots, chopped
- 2 zucchinis, seeded and chopped
- 4 cups mushrooms, stemmed and chopped
- Salt and pepper

Instructions

1. To the Multicooker mix in the chicken, chicken stock, 2 cups water, ginger and green onions. Press Manual and set timer to 30 minutes.
2. Add carrots, zucchini and mushrooms. Press Sauté mode and cook the veggies in the soup until tender.
3. Season the soup with salt and pepper. Serve immediately and enjoy!

Nutritional info (per serving): 282 calories; 11.5 g fat; 1 g total carbs; 42 g protein

Pancit

Cooking Time: 10 minutes

Servings: 6

Ingredients

- 1 bag (16 oz) rice sticks, soaked in water for 5 minutes, drained
- ½ lb pork, cooked, shredded
- 1 shallot, chopped
- 3 garlic cloves, minced
- 2 cups cabbage, shredded
- 2 cups carrots, sliced
- 4 cups chicken broth
- 2 tablespoons oil
- 3 tablespoons chicken seasoning
- 1 tablespoons oyster sauce
- 2 cups sweet peas

Instructions

1. Add 1 cup water and all the veggies to the Multicooker. Close the lid and press Manual, set the timer to 0. Once you hear the beep, do the quick release. Remove the veggies and clean the pot.
2. Add oil to the cooker and press Sauté button. Add shallot and garlic and cook for 1-2 minutes.
3. Add pork. Seasoning, oyster sauce and cook for 2 minutes. Add broth and rice sticks and stir well.
4. Close the lid and press Manual button, cook for 3 minutes. Do the quick release.
5. Add vegetables and stir well. Serve.

Nutritional info (Per serving): 464 calories; 35 g fat; 14 g total carbs; 22 g protein

Orange Chicken Lettuce Wraps

Cooking Time: 25 minutes

Servings: 6

Ingredients

- 32 oz. boneless skinless chicken breasts, cubed
- 2 tablespoons canola oil
- 1 tablespoon sesame oil
- 1 tablespoon rice vinegar
- 1/3 cup water
- ¼ cup soy sauce
- 1 teaspoon chile sauce
- 1 cup fresh orange juice
- 2 tablespoons brown sugar
- 1 tablespoon orange zest
- ¼ cup cornstarch
- Romaine lettuce leaves, for serving
- Cooked white rice, for serving

Instructions

1. Place the chicken in a shallow bowl. Coat with 2 tablespoons cornstarch.
2. Press the sauté function on the Multicooker and add oil.
3. Cook the chicken for about 5 minutes on each side for all the chicken.
4. Add water, soy sauce, sugar, vinegar, sesame oil, chili-garlic sauce, ½ cup orange juice and combine well to the Multicooker.
5. Cover tightly with the lid and position the vent to sealing. Press cancel button the press "Poultry" button, set timer to 7 minutes at high pressure. Let the pressure release naturally for 10 minutes.
6. Carefully remove lid, scoop some sauce and pour it in a mug. Stir in the cornstarch and return this mixture to the Multicooker. Press cancel to reset.
7. Press Sauté function and cook 5 minutes until the sauce thickens. Add in the orange juice, zest, salt and pepper to taste

8. Serve on the lettuce leaves and arrange them on a serving plate, top with rice and garnishes. Serve immediately and enjoy!

Nutritional info (per serving): 175 calories; 166.5 g fat; 70 g total carbs; 11 g protein

Filipino Edamame Spaghetti Squash

Cooking Time: 15 minutes

Servings: 6

Ingredients

- 3lbs. spaghetti squash
- 12 oz. shelled edamame
- 1 cup baby carrots
- ½ cup onions, chopped
- 2 oz. slivered almonds
- ½ cup cilantro, chopped
- 1 cup water
- 3 tablespoons lower sodium soy sauce
- 2 limes
- 4 teaspoons sugar
- 1 tablespoon ginger, grated
- 1/8 teaspoon crushed red pepper flakes

Instructions

1. Place the squash in a microwave safe shallow bowl and pierce it with a fork. Heat the microwave for about 2 minutes.
2. Remove from microwave, cut in half and scrape out the seeds.
3. Pour water into the Multicooker and place a metallic trivet.
4. Put the squash on the trivet, close lid tightly, close valve, press Manual/Pressure button in 7 minutes. Quick release pressure.
5. Whisk together soy sauce, juice of 1 lime, sugar ginger and pepper flakes in a medium bowl.
6. Remove the lid and take out the squash. Press cancel button to reset the Multicooker.
7. Press sauté mode, High and add the edamame to the hot water. Bring it to a boil for 2 minutes. Drain excess water.

8. Place the squash in a large bowl, run the fork around the outer edges to release the strands.
9. Serve the squash with edamame, carrots, green onion, soy sauce, nuts and cilantro.
10. Drizzle with remaining lime juice and enjoy!

Nutritional info (Per serving): 180 calories; 8 g fat; 21 g total carbs; 10 g protein

Lechon Asad

Cooking Time: 37 minutes

Servings: 4

Ingredients

- 6 lbs. pork shoulder, cubed
- 2 tablespoons olive oil
- 3 onions, 1 quartered the other two sliced
- 5 garlic cloves
- 3 cups Mojo Marinade

Instructions

1. Press the "Sauté" button on the Multicooker. Add olive oil.
2. Cook the pork until it is brown.
3. Add quartered onion, garlic and Mojo. Cover with lid and press "Meat/stew" button and cook for 30 minutes.
4. In the meantime, sauté the sliced onions in a small skillet over medium heat for about 5 minutes. Set the onions aside.
5. When pork is done, release the pressure quickly. Serve pork with sauce and sautéed onions. Enjoy!

Nutritional info (per serving): 134 calories; 7 g fat; 11 g total carbs; 4 g protein

Smoked Salmon Chowder

Cooking Time: 15 minutes

Servings: 6

Ingredients

- 2 ½ cups fish stock, warmed
- 1 lb. potatoes, diced
- 15 oz. can diced tomatoes, drained
- 4 oz. cream cheese, softened and sliced
- 1 cup heavy cream
- 4 oz. shrimp
- 8 oz. thick-cut smoked salmon, chopped
- 1 onion, diced
- 2 stalks celery, diced
- 6 cloves garlic, minced
- 3 tablespoons butter
- 1 teaspoon dried basil
- ¼ teaspoon fennel seeds, crushed
- 2 tablespoon tomato paste
- 2 tablespoon capers
- 2 bay leaves
- 1 tablespoon Old Bay seasoning

Instructions

1. Put the Multicooker on "Sauté" mode and add butter.
2. Add onions and celery. Sauté for 5 minutes, then add garlic, basil and fennel, cook for 2 minutes.
3. Add the stock and scrape the bottom so that nothing sticks to the bottom. Add potatoes, tomatoes, tomato paste, capers and bay leaves. Stir well.
4. Add the cream cheese on top and do not stir. Press Cancel, close the lid tightly and position the vent to sealing.

5. Press Manual and cook for 4 minutes. When done, release pressure naturally for 10 minutes, then do a quick release.
6. Add cream and old bay, stir well. Finally, fold in the shrimp and smoked salmon, press "Sauté" function on the Multicooker. Stir for 2 minutes.
7. Serve while hot with crusted bread. Enjoy!

Nutritional info (per serving): 336 calories; 19.7 g fat; 23 g total carbs; 17 g protein

Fish Chowder

Cooking Time: 15 minutes

Servings: 8

Ingredients

- 16 oz. potatoes, cubed
- 4 cups vegetable broth
- 1 cup frozen corn
- 1 cup heavy cream
- 16 oz. flaky white fish
- 1 6.5 oz. can clams, chopped
- 1 onion, chopped
- 4 celery stalks, chopped
- 2 tablespoons water
- 2 tablespoons cornstarch
- 1 teaspoon garlic powder
- 1 teaspoon dried thyme
- Salt, to taste

Instructions

1. Press Sauté button on the Multicooker, grease the pot with cooking spray. Add chopped onions, celery and potatoes.
2. Add the broth and corn. Add the flaky fish on top of the vegetables.
3. Close the lid, press Pressure cook button and press high, cook for about 5 minutes.
4. In a separate bowl, mix the water and cornstarch. Set aside.
5. Allow natural release of the pressure for 10 minutes. Press cancel button and carefully open the lid.
6. Press the Sauté button and bring mixture to a boil. Add the clams with their liquid and cornstarch mixture until mixture thickens. Press Cancel button.
7. Add heavy cream, garlic powder, thyme and salt. Mix well. Serve and enjoy!

Nutritional info (per serving): 231 calories; 14 g fat; 23 g total carbs; 17 g protein

Fish Biryani

Cooking Time: 55 minutes

Servings: 8

Ingredients

- 3 cups brown basmati rice, rinsed and drained
- 2 cups water
- 1 cup thin coconut milk
- 3 tablespoons ghee
- 1 onion, chopped
- 1 teaspoon ginger, grated
- 3 tomatoes seeded and diced
- Salt

Fish and Marinades:

- 2 lbs. boneless skinless firm white fish fillet, chopped
- ½ teaspoon turmeric powder
- 2 teaspoon chili powder
- Salt

Spices:

- 4 bay leaves
- 1 cinnamon stick
- 5 cloves
- 1 teaspoon turmeric powder
- 5 cardamom pods
- 1 teaspoon coriander powder
- 1 teaspoon garam masala

Instructions

1. Add the fish and its marinade to a container, cover and set aside for about 20 minutes.

2. Preheat the Multicooker by pressing the Sauté button; add ghee when the indicator shows hot.
3. Add onions and cook for 4 minutes. Add ginger and the spices and cook for 5 minutes.
4. Add the marinated fish pieces and cook on each side for about 2 minutes. Set fish aside.
5. Turn off sauté mode, add water, milk and stir well.
6. Add tomatoes and add the rice on top. Cover with lid, turn steam release valve to seal position, press "Pressure cook", high pressure and set the timer to 20 minutes. When done wait for 10 minutes. Turn the valve to venting position, let the pressure release quickly.
7. Fluff the rice and add the cooked fish on top. Serve and enjoy!

Nutritional info (per serving): 110 calories; 7.7 g fat; 8 g total carbs; 3 g protein

Chicken Macaroni Soup

Cooking Time: 10 minutes

Servings: 6

Ingredients

- 2 boneless skinless chicken thighs trimmed off excess fat, chopped
- 6 cups chicken broth
- 2 cups macaroni uncooked
- 4 cloves garlic peeled and bruised
- 2 carrots peeled and diced
- 1 cup sweet corn kernels
- 1 tablespoon chicken bouillon cube
- Salt, to taste

Instructions

1. Place all the ingredients except salt into the Multicooker.
2. Stir well, close the lid, turn the steam handle to sealing position
3. Press "Pressure cook", high pressure and set timer to 5 minutes. Quickly release the pressure.
4. Open the lid and season with salt to taste.
5. Meanwhile cook the macaroni according to package instructions. Drain and set aside.
6. Add the cooked macaroni to the soup. Serve while hot and enjoy!

Nutritional info (per serving): 158 calories; 14 g fat; 7 g total carbs; 3.3 g protein

Chicken and Dumplings

Cooking Time: 40 minutes

Servings: 5

Ingredients

- 1 cup diced onion
- ½ cup diced carrot
- ½ cup diced celery
- ½ cup frozen petite peas
- ½ cup frozen cut green beans
- 4 cups low-sodium chicken broth
- 1 lb. boneless, skinless chicken thighs
- 1 lb. bone-in chicken breasts, skin removed
- 1 bay leaf
- ½ tablespoon olive oil
- ½ teaspoon dried marjoram
- 2 tablespoons unsalted butter, softened
- 2 tablespoons all-purpose flour
- salt and ground black pepper

Dumplings:

- 1 cup all-purpose flour
- ½ cup buttermilk
- 1 teaspoon baking powder
- 2 tablespoons cold unsalted butter
- 1 tablespoon parsley, chopped
- Salt, to taste

Instructions

1. Press the Sauté mode on the Multicooker, add olive oil.
2. Cook the onions, carrots, celery and bay leaf for about 5 minutes.
3. Add chicken broth, chicken breasts and thighs, marjoram, salt and pepper. Close the lid, press "High pressure" and set the timer to 9 minutes.

4. Naturally release the pressure for 10 minutes. Then quick release for 5 minutes.
5. Remove chicken pieces and discard the bay leaf. In a separate bowl mix the butter with flour, set aside.
6. Combine flour, baking powder, and salt in a large bowl. Add in cold butter and parsley and mix well. Set it aside.
7. Shred the chicken and return to the Multicooker, add peas, green beans, flour-butter mixture and press Sauté mode, bring the mixture to a boil.
8. Add buttermilk to the dumpling mixture and mix well. Scoop the mixture and drop into the Multicooker.
9. Cover, leave the steam vent open, press slow cooker, and cook on low for about 12 minutes. When done remove from the Multicooker.
10. Serve while hot and enjoy!

Nutritional info (Per serving): 466 calories; 19.6 g fat; 29.2 g total carbs; 41.2 g protein

Noodle Bowls

Cooking Time: 15 minutes

Servings: 4

Ingredients

- ½ cup reduced sodium tamari soy sauce
- 2 cups chicken broth
- 16 oz. boneless, skinless chicken breast, chopped
- 8 ounces uncooked brown rice noodles
- 2 tablespoons rice vinegar
- 2 tablespoons almond butter
- 2 tablespoons erythritol
- 2 carrots, sliced
- Sliced green onions and chopped almonds, for topping

Instructions

1. Add all the ingredients to the Multicooker except the ones used for toppings.
2. Close the lid, turn the vent to sealing position, press Manual button and choose high pressure, set the timer for about 3 minutes. When the timer beeps, quickly release the pressure.
3. Remove the lid and stir the dish. Serve in 4 bowls topped with green onions and chopped almonds. Enjoy!

Nutritional info (Per serving): 430 calories; 8.8 g fat; 30 g total carbs; 32 g protein

Jambalaya Soup

Cooking Time: 20 minutes

Servings: 4

Ingredients

- 16 oz. Andouille Sausages, quartered lengthwise and chopped
- 3 boneless skinless chicken thighs, cubed
- 3 slices bacon, chopped
- 1 handful celery, chopped
- 1 medium carrot, sliced
- 1 onion, chopped
- 1 red bell pepper, chopped
- 3 tablespoon garlic powder
- 1 can diced tomatoes
- 2 cups rice
- 7 cups chicken broth
- ½ teaspoon Cajun powder
- ½ teaspoon cayenne pepper
- 2 bay leaves

Instructions

1. Preheat the Multicooker by pressing the Sauté button, add oil. Brown the bacon for 3 minutes and set aside.
2. Add the sausages and Cajun powder. Remove and set aside.
3. Add the chicken, season with salt, pepper and Cajun. Brown the chicken and set aside.
4. Sauté the onions, garlic, celery, carrots and peppers for about 4 minutes. Add tomatoes.
5. Add the rice and stir well to mix for 3 minutes.
6. Add chicken stock and bay leaves. Set to manual, high pressure for 12 minutes. When done do a quick release.
7. Serve and enjoy!

Nutritional info (Per serving): 210 calories; 6 g fat; 32 g carbs; 5 g protein

Clam Chowder

Cooking Time: 25 minutes

Servings: 4

Ingredients

- 3 6.5 oz cans chopped clams (reserve the clam juice)
- 1 ½ lbs. potatoes, diced
- 1 cup water
- 1 1/3 cups half and half
- 5 slices bacon, chopped
- 3 tablespoons butter
- 1 onion, diced
- 2 stalks celery, diced
- 2 sprigs fresh thyme
- 2 cloves garlic, minced
- ½ teaspoon sugar
- Salt and pepper, to taste

Instructions

1. Press Sauté function on the Multicooker and add the bacon, cook for 5 minutes.
2. Add butter, onion, celery and thyme and cook for 7 minutes.
3. Add garlic, salt and pepper and cook for a minute. Add potatoes, sugar, reserved clam juice and 1 cup water. Mix well.
4. Close the lid tightly, set the valve to sealing position, cancel Sauté function to reset the Multicooker. Choose Manual, press high pressure and set the timer to 4 minutes, then quickly release the pressure when done.
5. Remove the lid, use a fork to mash the potatoes, press Sauté mode. Add clams, half and half and let the chowder cook. Cook for about 5-6 minutes.
6. Serve and enjoy!

Nutritional info (Per serving): 254 calories; 13 g fat; 26 g total carbs; 34 g protein

Garlic Noodles

Cooking Time: 10 minutes

Servings: 3

Ingredients

- 8 oz. canton noodles
- 1 ¾ cup water
- 5 garlic cloves, minced
- 1 bell pepper, sliced
- 2 scallions, chopped
- 2 tablespoons oil
- ½ tablespoon soy sauce
- 1 tablespoon Schezwan Sauce
- 1 teaspoon vinegar
- Salt, to taste

Instructions

1. Combine oil, noodles, garlic, soy sauce, vinegar, schezwan sauce, water, bell peppers in the Multicooker. Make sure the noodles are submerged in water.
2. Close the lid, set the valve to sealing positions. Choose Manual, high pressure and set the timer to 4 minutes. Quickly release the pressure when done.
3. Season with salt to taste. Serve sprinkled with scallions. Enjoy!

Nutritional info (Per serving): 59 calories; 11 g fat; 59 g total carbs; 8 g protein

Corn on the Cob

Cooking Time: 5 minutes

Servings: 6

Ingredients

- 6 ears corns, dehusked
- 1 cup water
- 1 teaspoon lime zest
- 2 tablespoons cilantro, chopped
- Salt, to taste

Instructions

1. Add 1 cup of water to the cooker, place a metal trivet into the Multicooker.
2. Arrange the corn in two layers on the trivet.
3. Close the lid, turn the valve to sealing position, select Manual, high pressure and cook for 3 minutes. Quickly release the pressure when done.
4. Serve the corn topped with zest, cilantro and salt to taste. Enjoy!

Nutritional info (Per serving): 58 calories; 1 g fat; 10 g total carbs; 3 g protein

Fish Stew

Cooking Time: 20 minutes

Servings: 4

Ingredients

- ½ cup dry white wine
- 8 oz. bottled clam juice
- 2 ½ cups water
- ½ lb. potatoes, diced
- 15 oz. canned diced tomatoes
- 2 lbs. sea bass, chopped
- 4 tablespoons olive oil
- 1 onion, sliced
- 4 garlic cloves, chopped
- pinch crushed red pepper
- 2 tablespoons lemon juice
- 2 tablespoons fresh dill, chopped
- Salt and Pepper, to taste

Instructions

1. Press Sauté function on the Multicooker and add 2 tablespoons olive oil. Cook the onions for 3 minutes.
2. Add garlic and cook for ½ minute more. Add white wine and stir for 1 minute.
3. Add clam juice, water, potatoes, tomatoes, salt and pepper and crushed red pepper.
4. Close the lid, set the valve to sealing, press High pressure Manual and cook for about 5 minutes. Quick release pressure when done.
5. Press Sauté mode, add the fish and cook for 5 minutes until the fish is tender. Turn off the sauté mode.
6. Add lemon juice, dill and the remaining olive oil. Serve and enjoy!

Nutritional info (Per serving): 471 calories; 20 g fat; 24 g total carbs; 43 g protein

Easy Filipino Fried Rice

Cooking Time: 15 minutes

Servings: 4

Ingredients:

- 2 cups jasmine rice, washed and drained
- 1 cup diced bell peppers
- ½ small broccoli, cut into small florets
- 3 green onions, chopped
- 1 large carrot diced
- 2 tablespoons sesame oil
- 1 heaped tablespoon ginger-garlic paste
- 1 teaspoon sesame seeds
- 2 tablespoons soy sauce
- 1 tablespoon rice vinegar
- 1 ½ teaspoons corn flour
- 1 ½ tablespoons brown sugar
- salt

Instructions:

1. Add 1½ cups water to the Multicooker and insert a metal trivet.
2. To a steel bowl, add rice and 1 ½ cups water. Press Pressure Cook on High and cook for 6 minutes. When done do a quick release.
3. Take out rice and drain any excess liquid.
4. Put pot on Sauté mode. Press More.
5. Add sesame oil, ginger-garlic paste and sesame seeds and cook for a minute.
6. Add peppers, carrots and cook for 3 minutes.
7. Add broccoli and cook for 1 minute.
8. Add soy sauce, rice vinegar and cook for 2 minutes.
9. Add corn flour and stir to thicken the sauce.
10. Add brown sugar and jasmine. Combine thoroughly.
11. Press Cancel on the Multicooker, add green onions and salt to taste.

Nutritional info (per serving): 475 calories; 8 g fat; 89 g total carbs; 10 g protein

Steamed Crab Legs

Cooking Time: 5 minutes

Servings: 4

Ingredients:

- 2 lbs. wild-caught snow crab legs
- 1 cup water
- 1/3 cup salted grass-fed butter, melted
- lemon slices

Instructions:

1. Add 1 cup to the Multicooker and insert a metal trivet.
2. Add crab legs.
3. Close the lid, set valve to Sealed, press Manual button and set time for 3 minutes. Quick release when done.
4. Serve with butter and lemon slices.

Nutritional info (per serving): 282 calories; 11.5 g fat; 1 g total carbs; 42 g protein

Shrimp Fried Rice

Cooking Time: 25 minutes

Servings: 4

Ingredients:

- ½ lb. shrimp, peeled and deveined, tails left intact
- 1 cup onion, chopped
- 1 cup white basmati rice, rinsed and drained well
- 1 cup water
- 1 cup frozen peas
- 3 garlic cloves, minced
- 1 carrot, cubed
- 4 tablespoons vegetable oil, divided
- 2 large eggs
- 3 tablespoons soy sauce
- ½ teaspoon toasted sesame oil
- salt and pepper, to taste

Instructions:

1. Press Sauté function on the Multicooker. Add oil when hot.
2. Add all eggs and cook. Set aside in a bowl when done.
3. Add frozen peas and cook for 5 minutes, set aside when all water evaporates.
4. Add a tablespoon of oil to the Multicooker. Add shrimp and cook until pale pink, set aside.
5. Add the remaining oil, sauté onions and garlic for 2 minutes. Add rice and sauté for 20 seconds.
6. Add shrimp, carrots, water, salt and pepper. Close the lid, set valve to Sealed, press Cancel to reset the Multicooker.
7. Press "Rice" function, cook for 12 minutes, release pressure and press Cancel.
8. Open the lid, add eggs, peas, soy sauce, sesame oil and ground pepper.

Nutritional info (per serving): 336 calories; 19.7 g fat; 23 g total carbs; 17 g protein

Pork Shoulder Soup

Cooking Time: 50 minutes

Servings: 6

Ingredients:

- 3 lbs. pork shoulder trimmed of large fat pieces, cubed
- 1 lb. baby bok choy bottom stem removed and chopped
- 6 oz. fine egg noodles
- 1 cup dark soy sauce
- ¼ cup dark brown sugar packed
- ½ teaspoon crushed red pepper
- 5 cups chicken broth
- 8 dried shiitake mushrooms
- 4 green onions, chopped
- 8 cloves garlic, peeled
- 2 inches ginger, unpeeled and sliced
- 1 teaspoon Chinese Five Spice
- 1 teaspoon kosher salt
- 2 tablespoons sesame oil

Instructions:

1. Combine spices, soy sauce, brown sugar, sesame oil, broth, green onions, garlic and ginger into the Multicooker. Stir well.
2. Add cubed pork, close the lid, set valve to Sealed, press High pressure and cook for 45 minutes, release pressure naturally and remove the lid.
3. Scoop out mushrooms, ginger and garlic. Slice mushrooms and return to the Multicooker. Discard both garlic and ginger.
4. Add baby bok choy, close the lid, cook on High pressure for 1 minutes, release pressure and take the lid off.
5. Cook egg noodles separately according to package instructions and add to the soup.

Nutritional info (per serving): 447 calories; 16 g fat; 37 g total carbs; 37 g protein

Kabocha Squash Rice

Cooking Time: 10 minutes

Servings: 4

Ingredients:

- 2 cups Kabocha squash, cubed
- 1 ½ cup Japanese short grain rice, rinsed
- 1 ½ cup cold water
- 1 tablespoon Japanese rice wine
- 1 teaspoon sea salt
- 5 drops sesame oil

Instructions:

1. Combine rice, water, rice wine, sea salt and sesame oil in a Multicooker.
2. Add cubed squash.
3. Close the lid and cook on High pressure for 7 minutes. Naturally release pressure after 10 minutes.

Nutritional info (per serving): 341 calories; 10 g fat; 76 g total carbs; 6 g protein

Filipino Green Beans

Cooking Time: 5 minutes

Servings: 2

Ingredients:

- ½ lb. green beans
- ½ cup cold water
- salt and pepper

Instructions:

1. Add water to the Multicooker, place a steamer rack.
2. Place beans in the steamer rack.
3. Pressure cook on Low pressure for 0-2 minutes. Do a quick release.
4. Season with salt and pepper and serve.

Nutritional info (per serving): 108 calories; 7 g fat; 10 g total carbs; 2 g protein

Dinner

Filipino Style Picadillo

Cooking Time: 20 minutes

Servings: 4

Ingredients

- 1 lb. ground beef
- 1 cup water
- 1 cup raisins
- 1 cup peas
- 2 tomatoes, diced
- 3 potatoes, peeled and diced
- 2 carrots, peeled and diced
- 2 shallots, chopped
- 3 garlic cloves, minced
- 2 tablespoon olive oil
- 1 ½ tablespoon soy sauce
- 1 ½ tablespoon fish sauce
- Salt and pepper, to taste

Instructions

1. Press Sauté button on the Multicooker and add oil. Add shallots and garlic and cook for about 3 minutes.
2. Add beef and stir frequently until the meat browns. Add tomatoes and cook for 2 minutes more.
3. Add soy sauce, fish sauce, potatoes, carrots and 1 cup water. Close the lid and cook on Manual setting for 8 minutes.

4. Do the natural pressure release. Add the raisins and peas and heat for about 3 minutes.
5. Finally season the dish with salt and pepper. Serve and enjoy.

Nutritional info (Per serving): 144 calories; 12 g fat; 14 g total carbs; 21 g protein

Mung Bean Stew

Cooking Time: 30 minutes

Servings: 3

Ingredients

- ½ lb. ground pork
- 1 cup mung beans, rinsed
- 3 cups water
- 2 cups spinach, chopped
- ½ onion, diced
- 2 cloves garlic, minced
- 1 tablespoon coconut oil
- Salt, to taste

Instructions

1. Turn on the Multicooker and press sauté button. Add coconut oil
2. Sauté the onions and garlic for about 5 minutes
3. Add ground pork and cook for about 5 minutes, stirring the meat to break it down
4. Turn off sauté mode and add mung beans, water and spinach.
5. Cover with lid and cook on manual for 10 minutes.
6. When the timer beeps, release the pressure naturally. Serve and enjoy!

Nutritional info (Per serving): 231 calories; 15 g fat; 21 g total carbs; 12 g protein

Mechado Beef Stew with Coconut Milk and Salted Peanuts

Cooking Time: 1 hour 20 minutes

Servings: 4

Ingredients

- 4 cups boneless beef for stewing, cubed
- ¾ cup chicken broth
- ¾ cup coconut milk, plus extra for garnish
- ¼ cup roasted, salted peanuts, crushed
- 1 onion, chopped
- 2 unpeeled red potatoes, cubed
- 2 tablespoons corn oil
- 1 tablespoon all-purpose flour
- 1 teaspoon ground cumin
- ½ teaspoon ground ginger
- 1 pinch ground cinnamon
- 1 pinch cayenne pepper
- ¼ teaspoon Worcestershire sauce
- Salt and Pepper, to taste
- 1 fresh lime, quartered

Instructions

1. Combine flour, salt and pepper in a shallow bowl. Add the cubed meat and coat evenly. Set aside.
2. On the Multicooker press the sauté button and Normal mode, add 1 tablespoon oil and heat for 2 minutes.
3. Add the onion and cook for 5 minutes. Set the onions aside.
4. Add 1 tablespoon oil and wait for about 1 minute. Add beef, cumin, ginger, cinnamon and cayenne and cook for about 5 minutes.
5. Add the chicken stock and stir for about 1 minute. Add onions, potatoes and Worcestershire sauce. Combine well.

6. Close the lid, set the valve to sealing position, press cancel then press Manual and High Pressure. Set to 20 minutes.
7. When done, press the cancel button and release the pressure naturally for around 30 minutes. Add in the coconut milk.
8. Close the Multicooker for a few minutes. Season the stew with salt and pepper.
9. Serve with freshly squeezed lime juice and crushed peanuts. Enjoy!

Nutritional info (Per serving): 345 calories; 23 g fat; 15 g total carbs; 21 g protein

Filipino-Style Chicken Curry

Cooking Time: 20 minutes

Servings: 4

Ingredients

- 1 ½ lbs. chicken breasts, cubed
- ¼ cup chicken stock
- 1 13.5-ounce can full fat coconut milk
- 1 tablespoon fish sauce
- 1 ½ teaspoons ginger, grated
- 3 tablespoons red curry paste
- 1 tablespoon lime juice
- 1 teaspoon lime zest
- 1 tablespoon brown sugar
- 2 carrots, chopped
- 1 red bell pepper, chopped
- 1 yellow bell pepper, chopped
- 1 cup snow peas

Instructions

1. Add chicken stock, coconut milk, fish sauce, ginger, curry paste, lime juice, and lime zest to the Multicooker. Add chicken and coat well in the sauce.
2. Close the lid, press Manual cook function, high pressure and set the timer to 7 minutes
3. When done cooking and time is up, quickly release the pressure.
4. Remove chicken pieces and set aside. Add carrots, peppers and snow peas to the Multicooker.
5. Press the sauté button and bring the mixture to a boil. Continue to cook the vegies for about 4 minutes until soft.
6. Add the chicken pieces back to the Multicooker and cook for 5 minutes. Cancel the sauté mode.
7. Serve while hot with white rice. Enjoy!

Nutritional info (Per serving): 324 calories; 12g fat; 21 g total carbs; 22 g protein

Panang Curry

Cooking Time: 10 minutes

Servings: 6

Ingredients

- 14 oz. can coconut milk
- ¼ cup water
- ½ can maesri thai panang curry paste
- 1 cup baby corn, cut
- 1 cup carrots, chopped
- 1 lb. boneless skinless chicken thighs, chopped
- 1 cup broccoli florets
- 1 teaspoon fish sauce
- 1 teaspoon fresh lime juice

Instructions

1. To the Multicooker add the coconut milk and water. Turn the Multicooker to sauté mode.
2. Add curry paste and combine well. Add corn and carrots.
3. Add the chicken pieces to the Multicooker. Stir and bring to a simmer.
4. Close the lid and press cancel. Press manual and cook on high pressure for 3 minutes.
5. Quick release the pressure. Open the Multicooker and drizzle lime juice, stir well to mix.
6. Finally add broccoli and cook for less than 1 minute. Press sauté and cook for 1 minute
7. When done serve with rice and enjoy the dish!

Nutritional info (Per serving): 234 calories; 12g fat; 15 g total carbs; 12 g protein

Massaman

Cooking Time: 1 hour

Servings: 4

Ingredients

- 1 ½ lbs beef chuck, cut into 2-inch cubes
- 2 ½ cup coconut milk
- ½ onion, sliced thinly
- ¼ cup roasted peanuts
- 1 potato, diced
- 6 tablespoons massaman curry paste
- 3 tablespoons fish sauce
- 3 tablespoons palm sugar, chopped
- 3 tablespoons tamarind juice
- 2 tablespoons coconut oil

Instructions

1. Place a large skillet over medium high heat. Add coconut oil.
2. Add beef and let it sear until browned on both sides. Remove from heat and set aside.
3. Return skillet to medium heat and add water to coat the bottom of the pan. Scrape off the bottom of the pan and set the pan juices aside
4. Press sauté function on the Multicooker, medium heat, add coconut milk and bring it to a boil.
5. Whisk in curry paste, reduce heat to low and cook until it thickens.
6. Add remaining coconut milk, seared beef, pan juices, fish sauce, palm sugar and tamarind. Combine well.
7. Close the Multicooker, press Manual button and cook on high pressure for about 30 minutes. When timer beeps place a cold towel on top of the lid and let it cool for about 10 minutes.
8. Press quick release button and then carefully open the lid.
9. Add potatoes, onions and peanuts. Simmer on sauté function for about 15 minutes until the potatoes are tender.

10. When done serve over rice and enjoy!

Nutritional info (per serving): 282 calories; 11.5 g fat; 1 g total carbs; 42 g protein

Filipino Pork Chops Steak

Cooking Time: 1 hour 30 minutes

Servings: 4

Ingredients

- 1/2 cup + 1 tablespoon lemon juice
- ½ cup soy sauce
- 1 ½ cups organic broth (chicken, beef or vegetable)
- 3 pork chops, bone-in
- 1 onion, sliced
- 2 garlic cloves, minced
- 2 tablespoons vegetable oil
- Salt and pepper, to taste

Instructions

1. Place the pork chops in a shallow dish. Add 1 tablespoon lemon juice, salt and pepper, cover and set aside in the refrigerator for 1 hour.
2. Press Sauté button on the Multicooker and add oil. Sauté the onions for about 3 minutes.
3. Add garlic and chops to the pot and cook for 2 minutes per side. Add the remaining ingredients and stir well to combine.
4. Close the lid and cook on Manual high pressure for 20 minutes. Release the pressure naturally and serve!

Nutritional info (Per serving): 144 calories; 14 g fat; 3 g total carbs; 3 g protein

Chicken Afritada

Cooking Time: 30 minutes

Servings: 4

Ingredients

- 4 bone-in chicken thighs, with skin, rinsed and patted dry
- 1 4 ounce package sliced fresh mushrooms
- 1 14 ounce can stewed tomatoes
- ¾ cup water
- 3 stalks celery, chopped
- ½ onion, chopped
- 2 cloves garlic, minced
- 3 cubes chicken bouillon, crumbled
- 2 teaspoons herbes de Provence
- 2 tablespoons olive oil
- 2 tablespoons tomato paste
- 1 pinch red pepper flakes
- 1 pinch ground black pepper

Instructions

1. Place the Multicooker on sauté mode. Heat the oil in it.
2. Add chicken and cook for about 6 minutes on each side. Transfer chicken to a separate bowl;
3. To the Multicooker add celery, mushrooms and onions cook for about 5 minutes; Add garlic and cook for 2 minutes more.
4. Add chicken, tomatoes and tomato paste to the Multicooker. Mix well then drizzle herbes de Provence.
5. Add water and bouillon. Close tightly with lid, press high pressure and cook for 11 minutes.
6. When done, do a quick release for 5 minutes, and carefully remove lid. Season with red chili pepper flakes and black pepper.
7. Serve and enjoy!

Nutritional info (Per serving): 392 calories; 24.5 g fat; 13.6 g total carbs; 29.9 g protein

Ginger Soy Chicken

Cooking Time: 18 minutes

Servings: 3

Ingredients

- 1 ½ lbs. chicken wings and drumsticks, chopped
- 1 tablespoon oil
- 1-inch piece ginger, peeled and sliced
- 2 tablespoons soy sauce
- 3 tablespoons sweet soy sauce
- 3 dashes ground white pepper
- ½ cup water
- 1 teaspoon sesame oil
- 1 stalk scallion, chopped

Instructions

1. Press sauté function on the Multicooker. When heated add oil and sear the chicken until slightly browned on both sides.
2. Add ginger and cook for 3 minutes. Add soy sauce, sweet soy sauce, ground white pepper, sesame oil and water.
3. Seal the Multicooker, press manual, High pressure for 8 minutes.
4. When the timer goes off, quick release and carefully remove the lid.
5. Add scallions and serve. Enjoy dish!

Nutritional info (Per serving): 409 calories; 26 g fat; 19 g total carbs; 24 g protein

Sticky Ribs

Cooking Time: 45 minutes

Servings: 4

Ingredients

- 1 rack baby back pork ribs back membrane removed
- 2 stalks scallions, chopped
- 1 tablespoon sesame seeds

Spice Rub:

- 1 ½ tablespoon chili powder
- 1 teaspoon cinnamon
- 1 ½ teaspoon ginger powder
- 1 ½ teaspoon coriander powder
- 1 ½ Tablespoon brown sugar
- 1 ½ teaspoon smoked paprika
- 1 ½ teaspoon salt
- 1 ½ teaspoon pepper
- 1 ½ teaspoon onion powder
- 1 ½ teaspoon garlic powder
- 1 ½ teaspoon dried parsley

For the Sauce:

- 1 cup water
- ¼ cup rice vinegar
- 2-inch ginger, sliced
- 3 cloves garlic, smashed

Instructions

1. In a medium bowl combine all the spice rub ingredients. Rub and coat the ribs with spice mixture. Set aside.

2. Add the sauce ingredients to the Multicooker. Add metal trivet inside and place ribs on it.
3. Press Manual setting, cook on High pressure for 25 minutes. When done wait for 10 minutes, and then do a quick release.
4. Preheat oven to broil. Place ribs on a rack with a parchment lined sheet pan.
5. Brush the ribs with soy glaze and place in the oven. Broil for 6 minutes. Remove from oven.
6. Serve with scallions and sesame seeds. Enjoy!

Nutritional info (Per serving): 381 calories; 24 g fat; 11 g total carbs; 28 g protein

Filipino-Style Pork Belly

Cooking Time: 30 minutes

Servings: 8

Ingredients

- 40 oz. pork belly, chopped
- 1 cup rose-flavored rice wine
- 1 cup light soy sauce
- ¾ cup dark soy sauce
- ½ cup sugar
- 5 cups water
- 5 slices ginger
- 2 scallions, chopped
- 3 star anise
- 1 tablespoon olive oil
- Salt, to taste

Instructions

1. Press the sauté function on the Multicooker. Add olive oil.
2. Cook the ginger for ½ a minutes. Add scallions and cook for 1 minute.
3. Add star anise, rice wine, light soy sauce, dark soy sauce, sugar, water and salt.
4. Close the lid tightly, set vent, press high pressure and cook for 5 minutes then quick release pressure.
5. Open the lid and add the pork belly, set to high pressure and cook for 20 minutes. When timer beeps allow pressure to release naturally.
6. Remove the pork and cut it. Serve over rice and drizzle sauce on top. Enjoy dish!

Nutritional info (Per serving): 776 calories; 77 g fat; 4 g total carbs; 14 g protein

Filipino Spaghetti Sauce

Cooking Time: 15 minutes

Servings: 4

Ingredients

- 4 cups lean ground beef
- 1 24 oz. marinara sauce
- 36 oz water
- 1 14.5 oz canned diced tomatoes
- ½ teaspoon salt
- ½ teaspoon garlic powder
- ½ teaspoon onion powder
- ½ teaspoon Italian Seasoning
- 1 spaghetti pack

Instructions

1. Press Sauté function on the Multicooker.
2. Add beef, salt, garlic powder, onion powder and Italian seasoning. Cook the meat while stirring frequently until well browned. Turn off the Multicooker.
3. Place the spaghetti on top of the ground meat.
4. Add spaghetti sauce, diced tomato and water to the Multicooker.
5. Set to Manual, high pressure and cook for 8 minutes. When the pot beeps, quickly release the pressure and open the pot. Stir the dish.
6. Serve immediately and enjoy!

Nutritional info (Per serving): 385 calories; 4 g fat; 56 g total carbs; 26 g protein

Chicken Paws

Cooking Time: 1hour 35 minutes

Servings: 6

Ingredients

- 24 oz. chicken feet, cleaned
- 3 tablespoons oil
- 1 ¾ cups chicken broth

For the Marinade:

- ¼ teaspoon kosher salt
- ½ teaspoon black pepper
- 1 Tablespoon soy sauce
- 1 tablespoon fish sauce
- 1 tablespoon rice vinegar
- 1 tablespoon sugar
- ¼ teaspoon liquid smoke

For the Sauce:

- 3 tablespoons Soy sauce
- 1 tablespoon hoison sauce
- 2 tablespoons Gochujang
- 1 tablespoon Sesame oil
- 3 cloves garlic
- 1 ginger
- 1 tablespoon sugar
- ¼ cup chicken broth

Instructions

1. Add the chicken feet to a container, add the marinade ingredients to the container. Set aside to marinate for about 1-2 hours.
2. Put the Multicooker to "Sauté" mode and add oil.

3. Add the chicken feet to the pot and do not discard the marinade. Pour the marinade to a bowl and add the sauce ingredients. Mix well.
4. Cook the chicken feet until browned and add chicken broth, stir well so that nothing sticks to the bottom.
5. Set to pressure cook for 20 minutes. Release the pressure naturally for 10 minutes then quick release.
6. Remove from the Multicooker. Serve immediately and enjoy!

Nutritional info (per serving): 175 calories; 7.7 g fat; 24.5 g total carbs; 4.7 g protein

Chicken with Paprika and Butternut Squash

Cooking Time: 15 minutes

Servings: 2

Ingredients

- 17.6 oz. chicken thigh fillets
- 17.6 oz. butternut squash, peeled and diced
- 1 onion, sliced
- 3 garlic cloves, chopped
- 2 tablespoons Worcestershire sauce
- 1 tablespoon olive oil
- 2 tablespoons paprika sweet
- 1 ½ tablespoons dried parsley

Instructions

1. Add the olive oil and chicken to the Multicooker, choose the Sauté mode.
2. Add onions, garlic, Worcestershire sauce and mix well making sure nothing sticks to the bottom. Press cancel to reset the Multicooker.
3. Add butternut squash, paprika and parsley. Mix well.
4. Lock the lid tightly, position vent to sealing, press pressure cook and set to 5 minutes.
5. When done, do a natural pressure release. Serve and enjoy!

Nutritional info (per serving): 294 calories; 12.6 g fat; 41 g total carbs; 2.6 g protein

Beef Potato Curry

Cooking Time: 1 hour

Servings: 6

Ingredients

- 2 ½ lbs. beef stew meat, chopped
- 1 lb. small potatoes, halved
- 1/3 cup cooking oil
- ½ cup water
- 1 tomato, diced
- 1 onion diced
- 2 tablespoon ginger, grated
- 4 cloves garlic, minced
- 1 teaspoon sugar
- Salt

Spices:

- 2 tablespoons turmeric powder
- 1 tablespoon Madras curry powder
- 1 teaspoon cumin powder
- 1 large cinnamon stick
- 2 tablespoons paprika
- 2 bay leaves
- 2 lime, cut into wedges

Instructions

1. Preheat the Multicooker by pressing Sauté button. Add oil.
2. Add onion, ginger and garlic and cook for 3 minutes.
3. Add tomato pieces, turmeric, curry, cumin, cinnamon and paprika. Cook for 2 minutes.
4. Add beef, bay leaves, sugar and salt. Mix well.
5. Add ½ cup water, close lid tightly, turn vent to sealing position, press the Multicooker, high pressure and timer to 30 minutes. Release the pressure quickly when done.

6. Remove the lid, cancel and press sauté function. Add potatoes and cook for 20 minutes. Turn it off.
7. Serve with lemon wedges and enjoy!

Nutritional info (per serving): 166 calories; 9 g fat; 20 g total carbs; 2.2 g protein

Kaffir Chicken

Cooking Time: 20 minutes

Servings: 6

Ingredients

- 3 lbs. bone-in skin-on drumettes and wings
- 1 cup water
- 1 cup coconut cream
- ¼ cup curry leaves
- 3 tomatoes, halved
- 1 onion peeled, sliced
- 3 cloves garlic, diced
- 6 kaffir Lime leaves tear the edges to release flavor
- 2 tablespoons cooking oil
- 1 tablespoon turmeric powder
- 1 small star anise
- 1 tablespoon paprika powder
- Salt, to taste

Instructions

1. Press "Sauté" function on the Multicooker. Add oil.
2. Add onions, garlic, paprika and cook for 1 minute. Add star anise, curry leaves, kaffir lime leaves, turmeric and cook for another minute.
3. Add chicken, water and tomatoes. Close lid, turn steam release to sealed position, press "Pressure cook" and set the timer to 15 minutes.
4. When done, naturally release the pressure, making sure all pressure is released.
5. Remove the lid carefully and add coconut cream. Season with salt and serve immediately. Enjoy!

Nutritional info (per serving): 255 calories; 15.4 g fat; 20.3 g total carbs; 5 g protein

Soy Sauce Braised Pork

Cooking Time: 1 hour 30 minutes

Servings: 6

Ingredients

- 3 lbs. pork belly with skin, patted dry
- ½ teaspoon five-spice powder
- 2 cups water
- 1 large onion peeled and diced
- 5 cloves garlic
- 1 medium cinnamon stick
- 1 star anise

Seasonings:

- ¼ cup soy sauce
- 1/3 cup dark soy sauce
- 1/3 cup Chinese rock sugar
- 1/3 cup brown sugar
- ¼ teaspoon ground white pepper

Instructions

1. Place the pork on a large plate and rub it with the five spice powder. Set aside for ½ an hour.
2. Place the pork into the Multicooker, add water, garlic, cinnamon, anise, seasonings ingredients and cover tightly with the lid.
3. Turn valve to seal, set the Multicooker to high pressure and set the timer to 45 minutes. When timer is off, release the pressure naturally.
4. Place on a large plate and let it cool. Slice and serve over noodles or rice. Enjoy!

Nutritional info (per serving): 271 calories; 16.7 g fat; 27 g total carbs; 3.5 g protein

Lu Rou Fan

Cooking Time: 35 minutes

Servings: 4

Ingredients

- 1 ½ lbs. pork belly with skin on
- 2 cups hot water
- 6 hard-boiled eggs peeled
- 4 cloves garlic, minced
- 1 cinnamon
- 2 slices ginger
- 2 star anise
- 1/3 cup fried shallots
- 1 teaspoon cooking oil
- 2 tablespoons corn starch + 3 tablespoons of water

  Seasonings:

- ¼ cup Shaoxing wine
- ¼ cup brown sugar
- 3 tablespoons dark soy sauce
- 2 tablespoons light soy sauce

Instructions

1. Press the Sauté function on the Multicooker, add the cooking oil.
2. Add the pork belly and cook for 5 minutes. Add ginger, garlic, cinnamon, anise and hot water. Mix well.
3. Add the hard boiled eggs. Cover tightly with the lid, turn the valve to seal, set the "Multicooker" to high pressure and set the timer to 30 minutes. When done and timer beeps, release the pressure naturally.
4. Turn to Sauté mode and bring mixture to a boil, add cornstarch mixture and cook until thick. Turn off the sauté mode. Serve immediately and enjoy!

Nutritional info (per serving): 249 calories; 23 g fat; 7 g total carbs; 7 g protein

Arroz Caldo with Chicken

Cooking Time: 40 minutes

Servings: 5

Ingredients

- 10 pieces of chicken wingettes
- 10 cloves of garlic, minced
- 1 onion, chopped
- 1 tablespoon ginger, sliced
- 1 cup jasmine rice, uncooked
- 1 pint of chicken broth
- 2 tablespoon fish sauce
- 2 tablespoon vegetable oil
- Lemon wedges

Instructions

1. Press "Sauté" function on the Multicooker. Add oil, garlic, onions and ginger. Cook for 5 minutes.
2. Add chicken and cook for 5 minutes until it is brown.
3. Add fish sauce, rice and chicken broth. Mix well and close the Multicooker, press "Porridge" function and cook on high for about 25 minutes.
4. When done, quick release the pressure. Serve with lemon wedges and enjoy!

Nutritional info (Per serving): 168 calories; 11 g fat; 15 g total carbs; 22 g protein

Chicken Adobo and Gravy

Cooking Time: 30 minutes

Servings: 2

Ingredients

- 2 medium boneless, skinless chicken breasts
- 1 cup chicken stock
- 2 tablespoons cold water + 2 tablespoons cornstarch
- 1 tablespoon olive oil
- ¾ teaspoon paprika
- ½ teaspoon thyme
- ¼ teaspoon garlic powder
- A pinch of sage
- Salt and black pepper, to taste

Instructions

1. In a medium bowl mix ½ teaspoon salt, paprika, thyme, pepper, garlic powder and sage. This makes the seasoning.
2. Place the chicken on a shallow bowl and rub with the seasonings.
3. Press Sauté function on the Multicooker, high heat. Add oil.
4. Cook the chicken for 3 minutes until browned on all sides. Add chicken to a bowl and set aside.
5. Add chicken stock, turn off the Multicooker and place a metal trivet into the Multicooker. Arrange chicken breasts on top.
6. Close lid, press high pressure and set timer to 5 minutes. Release the pressure naturally for 10 minutes, do a quick release for 5 minutes, place the chicken on a plate and cover with foil to keep it warm. Set aside.
7. Add the cornstarch mixture in to the Multicooker, press Sauté function. Cook while stirring to thicken the gravy.
8. Season with salt and pepper. Remove from the cooker. Serve chicken and drizzle gravy on top.

Nutritional info (Per serving): 418 calories; 14 g fat; 9.1 g total carbs; 59.8 g protein

Filipino Steak Chops

Cooking Time: 1 hour

Servings: 4

Ingredients

- 1/3 cup fresh calamansi Juice
- ½ cup soy sauce
- ½ cup water
- 6 pork chops
- 2 onions
- 1 tablespoon brown sugar
- 2 tablespoons olive oil
- Black pepper, to taste

Instructions

1. Add the pork chops to a container, add the calamansi juice, soy sauce and let it marinate for about 30 minutes.
2. Press the sauté button on the Multicooker and preheat it.
3. When hot, add in the olive oil. Sauté the pork chops for 5 minutes then set aside.
4. Sauté the onions in the Multicooker, add in water and the marinade. Add brown sugar and mix well.
5. Add the pork chops, press cancel to reset the Multicooker. Close the lid.
6. Press "Meat" function and cook for 10 minutes. Naturally release the pressure when done. Serve while hot and enjoy!

Nutritional info (Per serving): 312 calories; 11 g fat; 8 g total carbs; 18 g protein

Creamy Lemon Garlic Chicken

Cooking Time: 20 minutes

Servings: 4

Ingredients

- 4 chicken breasts
- 1 cup potatoes, cubed
- ½ cup Parmesan
- ½ cup heavy cream
- 2 cups chicken stock
- 1 large carrot, cubed
- 2 tablespoons fresh lemon juice
- 1 teaspoon lemon zest
- 1 tablespoon garlic, chopped
- 2 tablespoons cornstarch + 1 tablespoon water
- 1 tablespoon paprika
- 1 teaspoon garlic powder
- Salt and pepper, to taste

Instructions

1. Place the chicken in a shallow bowl, season with paprika, garlic powder, salt and pepper.
2. Place the chicken in the Multicooker, press the sauté function and sear the chicken for about 3 minutes on each side. Take it out and set aside.
3. Sauté the potatoes, carrots, salt and pepper in the Multicooker, remove and set aside.
4. Add chicken stock to the Multicooker, Parmesan, chopped garlic, lemon zest, lemon juice, heavy cream, chicken, potatoes and carrots. Press Cancel to reset the Multicooker then press "Poultry" for 8 minutes.
5. Release pressure quickly, take out the chicken meat and place into a greased baking sheet, set the oven to broil and broil the chicken for 3 minutes.
6. Add the potatoes and carrots to the chicken.
7. Add the cornstarch mixture to the Multicooker and stir to thicken. Remove from the Multicooker.

8. Serve chicken with potatoes and carrots and drizzle the thick sauce on it. Enjoy!

Nutritional info (Per serving): 168 calories; 11 g fat; 15 g total carbs; 22 g protein

Ilonggo Pork Spare

Cooking Time: 40 minutes

Servings: 4

Ingredients

- 2 lbs. pork spare ribs, cut into pieces
- ½ cup rice wine vinegar
- ¼ cup soy sauce
- 6 cloves garlic, crushed
- 1 shallot, sliced
- 5 bay leaves
- 2 tablespoons vegetable oil
- 1 tablespoon whole peppercorn
- 2 tablespoons white sugar
- 1 tablespoon annatto seeds

Instructions

1. Set the Multicooker to the "Sauté" mode. Add vegetable oil and annatto.
2. Sauté for ½ a minute, turn it off and take out the seeds.
3. Press Sauté function on the Multicooker add ribs and brown for about 4 minutes.
4. Add the garlic, shallots, peppercorn, bay leaves, vinegar, soy sauce and sugar. Combine, close lid, set Manual, press high pressure and cook for 15 minutes.
5. Naturally release pressure for 10 minutes, then release the remaining pressure, open the lid and press Sauté mode and let it cook for 15 minutes.
6. Remove from the Multicooker and serve immediately. Enjoy!

Nutritional info (Per serving): 464 calories; 20.5 g fat; 63.5 g total carbs; 13.5 g protein

Garlic Beef

Cooking Time: 1 hour 20 minutes

Servings: 6

Ingredients

- 3 lbs. chuck roast, cut to quarters and trimmed of all excess fat
- ½ cup white distilled vinegar
- ½ cup low sodium soy sauce
- 6 garlic cloves, crushed
- 1 ½ tsp whole black peppercorns
- 3 bay leaves

Instructions

1. Put the roast into the Multicooker. Add vinegar, soy sauce, garlic, peppercorns, and bay leaves.
2. Cover with the lid, set the valve to sealing, press pressure cook for 1 hour 10 minutes. Naturally release pressure.
3. Remove the roast and place on a chopping board. Set the pot to Sauté mode and let the sauce cook for 7 more minutes.
4. Shred the roast and return meat to the pot. Serve and enjoy!

Nutritional info (Per serving): 237 calories; 8.6 g fat; 2.2 g total carbs; 35 g protein

Monggo Curry

Cooking Time: 20 minutes

Servings: 2

Ingredients

- 4 tablespoons canola oil
- 1 tablespoon whole cumin seeds
- 3 tablespoons garlic, crushed
- 14 oz. can crushed tomatoes
- 2 tablespoons ginger, grated
- 2 tablespoons ground coriander
- 1 teaspoon turmeric powder
- 1 teaspoon cayenne pepper
- 3 cups water
- 1 cup mung beans, rinsed
- 14 oz. can coconut milk
- ½ cup fresh cilantro, chopped
- 3 tablespoons lime juice

Instructions

1. Preheat the Multicooker by pressing the Sauté function. Add oil and cumin seeds and cook for 1 minute.
2. Add garlic and cook for 4 minutes. Add tomatoes, ginger, coriander, turmeric, salt and cayenne. Cook for 5 minutes.
3. Add 3 cups water and mung beans, close lid, set to Manual, choose high pressure, cook for about 10 minutes
4. Release the pressure naturally and remove the lid. Add coconut milk, lime juice and cilantro.
5. Serve and enjoy!

Nutritional info (Per serving): 192 calories; 15.8 g fat; 7 g total carbs; 8 g protein

Paksiw Na Lechon

Cooking Time: 35 minutes

Servings: 4

Ingredients

- 3 cups lechon (roast pork belly), cubed
- 5 cups Filipino lechon sauce (liver sauce)
- ¼ cup cider vinegar
- 2 cups beef broth
- 4 cloves garlic peeled, minced
- 3 pieces bay leaves
- 1 teaspoon black peppercorns
- ½ cup brown sugar
- Salt, to taste

Instructions

1. Combine the pork cubes, Lechon sauce, vinegar, broth, garlic, bay leaves, peppercorns, salt and sugar in the Multicooker, do not mix.
2. Close the lid, set the valve to sealing, press Manual, high pressure and set the timer to 25 minutes.
3. Do a quick release, open the lid and stir well.
4. Serve over rice and enjoy!

Nutritional info (Per serving): 264 calories; 2 g fat; 58 g total carbs; 4 g protein

Filipino Pork Pata Tim

Cooking Time: 1 hour 50 minutes

Servings: 8

Ingredients

- 4 lbs pork pata (hock, knuckles, trotters); bone-in cut into serving pieces
- ¼ cup soy sauce
- 6 cups organic chicken broth
- ½ cup brown sugar
- 1 tablespoon lemon juice
- 2 tablespoons vegetable oil
- 2 cloves garlic peeled, mashed
- 1 whole white or yellow onion chopped
- 3 star anise points
- 2 pieces bay leaves
- ½ teaspoon black peppercorns
- Salt, to taste

Instructions

1. Place the pork into a shallow bowl and add soy sauce and lemon juice. Cover and let it marinate in the refrigerator for 60 minutes.
2. Add oil to the Multicooker and press Sauté button.
3. Add garlic, pata, onions, star anise, brown sugar, bay leaves, peppercorns, salt and broth. Do not mix.
4. Close the lid tightly, valve set to sealing, press Manual, high pressure and cook for 45 minutes. Do a quick release when the timer goes off.
5. Open the lid and stir well. Serve immediately and enjoy!

Nutritional info (Per serving): 74 calories; 7 g fat; 2 g total carbs; 2 g protein

Cashew Adobo Chicken

Cooking Time: 15 minutes

Servings: 4

Ingredients

- 1 ¼ lbs. chicken thighs, chopped
- 2 tablespoons coconut oil
- 3 ½ cups broccoli florets
- 1 red bell pepper, chopped
- 1 tablespoon arrowroot starch +2 tablespoons water
- Salt and pepper

Sauce and marinade
- 6 tablespoons tamari
- 1 tablespoon hoisin sauce
- 1 teaspoons toasted sesame oil
- 2 teaspoons coconut sugar
- ¾ tablespoon apple cider vinegar
- ½ teaspoon ginger, minced
- 2 garlic cloves, minced
- ½ cup chicken broth

Instructions

1. Mix tamari, hoisin sauce, sesame oil, coconut sugar, vinegar, ginger and garlic in a medium bowl, set aside.
2. Add the chicken to a shallow bowl and season with salt, pepper and 1 tablespoon of the marinade. Set aside to marinate.
3. Press Sauté mode on the Multicooker and add oil. Add chicken and cook for 2 minutes. Add broth.
4. Set the valve to sealing, press Manual and cook for 4 minutes. When done do a quick release.
5. Unlock the lid, press sauté mode, add arrowroot starch mixture to the pot.
6. Add cashews and veggies and cook until sauce thickens. Remove from the Multicooker.
7. Serve and enjoy!

Nutritional info (Per serving): 255 calories; 15.4 g fat; 20.3 g total carbs; 5 g protein

Coconut Pork

Cooking Time: 40 minutes

Servings: 8

Ingredients

- 1 tablespoon coconut oil
- ½ onion, chopped
- 3 tablespoons turmeric, grated
- 2 tablespoons ginger, grated
- 3 cloves garlic, minced
- ½ teaspoon cinnamon
- ¼ teaspoon cardamom
- 1 cup crushed canned tomatoes
- 1 can 15oz. full fat coconut milk
- 6 pieces boneless pork shoulder, chopped

For the Turmeric Ginger Rice:
- 1 cup dry white rice
- 2 cups chicken broth
- 1/3 cup chopped dried fruit (apricots, cherries, cranberries, etc.)
- ¼ cup sliced almonds
- 1 tablespoon turmeric, grated
- 1 tablespoon ginger, grated

Instructions

1. Press Sauté button on the Multicooker. Add coconut oil. Cook the onions for 5 minutes.
2. Add turmeric, ginger, garlic, cardamom, cinnamon, salt and pepper. Cook for about 50 seconds while stirring frequently.
3. Add tomatoes, coconut milk and pork. Close the lid, set the valve to sealing, press Meat function and cook for 30 minutes.
4. Release the pressure naturally, open the lid and take out the pork pieces and shred the meat.
5. Press Sauté mode and bring mixture to a simmer. Add the shredded pork back and press Keep warm while preparing the rice.

6. Place a small pot over medium heat. Add rice, broth, turmeric and ginger, bring it to a boil then reduce the heat and let it cook until all broth is absorbed.
7. Add dried fruit and nut. Serve with pork and enjoy!

Nutritional info (Per serving): 575 calories; 40 g fat; 18 g total carbs; 36 g protein

Filipino Inspired Steamed Ginger Scallion Fish

Cooking Time: 1 hour

Servings: 4

Ingredients:

- Mix and Marinade:
- 3 tablespoons soy sauce
- 2 tablespoon rice wine
- 1 tablespoons Chinese black bean paste
- 1 teaspoon minced ginger
- 1 teaspoon garlic
- 1 lb. firm white fish
- 1 tablespoon peanut oil

Vegetables:

- 2 tablespoons julienned ginger
- ¼ cup green onions
- ¼ cup chopped cilantro
- ¼ cup chopped Scallions

Instructions:

1. Mix sauce ingredients in a medium bowl. Set aside
2. Place fish pieces in a shallow bowl and pour sauce over it. Set aside to marinate for 30 minutes to one hour.
3. Add 2 cups water to the Multicooker.
4. Add steamer and put fish pieces on the steamer, do not discard the marinade.
5. Cook fish on low pressure, and then release pressure when done cooking.
6. Place a small skillet over medium heat and add oil.
7. Sauté ginger for 10 seconds.
8. Add scallions and cilantro. Add reserved marinade and bring to a boil.
9. Serve fish and drizzle the marinade sauce on top.

Nutritional info (per serving): 171 calories; 5 g fat; 4 g total carbs; 24 g protein

Honey Garlic Shrimp

Cooking Time: 20 minutes

Servings: 4

Ingredients:

- 1 lb. frozen raw shrimp, shell on
- 1 cup water

Honey garlic sauce:

- 2 teaspoons vegetable oil
- 1 tablespoon garlic, minced
- 1 tablespoon ginger, minced
- 1/3 cup soy sauce
- ¼ cup honey
- ½ teaspoon cornstarch + 1 teaspoon water
- 1 tablespoon green onion, minced

Instructions:

1. Add water to the Multicooker and place a steamer basket.
2. Put shrimp in the basket and lock.
3. Press Manual, pressure cook on High and cook for 15 minutes. When done, do a quick release and open the lid.
4. Set shrimp aside and drain excess liquid.
5. Press Sauté function on the Multicooker. Add oil.
6. Sauté garlic and ginger for 1 minute.
7. Add soy sauce and honey, bring it to a boil.
8. Add cornstarch mixture to thicken sauce. Add shrimp to coat it with sauce.
9. Serve with green onions.

Nutritional info (per serving): 212 calories; 36 g fat; 20 g total carbs; 24 g protein

Mechado Filipino Beef Stew

Cooking Time: 2 hours 30 minutes

Servings: 4

Ingredients:

- 1 ½ lbs. beef for stew
- ¼ cup good dark soy sauce
- 1 cup tomato sauce
- 1 ½ cups water
- 3 cups beef stock
- 1 red bell pepper sliced
- 2 potatoes peeled and chopped
- 2 carrots peeled and chopped
- 3 cloves garlic minced or crushed
- 1 onion, diced
- half a lemon juiced
- 3 tablespoons canola oil
- 1 teaspoon fish sauce
- several dashes of tabasco
- 2 bay leaves
- kosher salt and pepper

Instructions:

1. Mix soy sauce, lemon and black pepper in a small bowl.
2. Place meat in a container and pour soy sauce marinade on top. Set aside for ½ hour.
3. Place a large skillet over medium heat, add garlic and cook until it browns and set aside.
4. Add beef and do not discard the marinade.
5. Add fish sauce, onions and cook for 5 minutes.
6. Add tomato sauce and water, cook for 2 minutes.

7. Add tabasco, beef stock, 2 tablespoons reserved marinade, bay leaves and pepper. Bring the mixture to a boil. Lower heat and let it simmer.
8. Add garlic, cover and let it simmer for 90 minutes.
9. Add potatoes, carrots and cook for 20 minutes.
10. Season with salt and pepper, Remove from the heat before serving.

Nutritional info (per serving): 567 calories; 24 g fat; 32 g total carbs; 54 g protein

Soy Sauce Chicken Rice

Cooking Time: 15 minutes

Servings: 4

Ingredients:

- 8 bone-in chicken legs
- 1 tablespoon dark soy sauce
- 1 cup jasmine rice
- 1 cup cold water

Master stock mixture:

- 3 tablespoons regular soy sauce
- 1/2 tablespoon dark soy sauce
- 4 cloves garlic, crushed
- 3 star anise
- ½ teaspoon sichuan pepper
- ¾ cup cold water

Instructions:

1. Add the master stock mixture ingredients to the Multicooker.
2. Add chicken legs.
3. Place a metal trivet in the Multicooker and add a steamer rack.
4. Mix rice and water in a stainless steel bowl and place this bowl in the steamer.
5. Close the lid, set valve to Sealed, pressure cook on High pressure for 8 minutes. Naturally release the pressure for 10 minutes and open the lid.
6. In a separate bowl, mix 1 tablespoon dark soy sauce with 1 tablespoon master stock.
7. Serve chicken and rice with soy sauce.

Nutritional info (per serving): 782 calories; 41 g fat; 50 g total carbs; 47 g protein

Pinoy Whole Chicken

Cooking Time: 25 minutes

Servings: 4

Ingredients:
- 2.8 lb whole chicken
- 1 onion, chopped
- 15 garlic cloves, minced
- ¼ cup fish sauce
- ¼ cup calamansi juice
- ½ teaspoon brown sugar
- 1 teaspoon each salt and pepper
- 6 lemongrass stalks
- 3 bay leaves

Instructions:
1. Combine garlic, fish sauce, calamansi juice, sugar, salt and pepper in a bowl.
2. Rub the chicken with the mixture and place into the dish that will fit into the Multicooker.
3. Add onion. Place the trivet inside the Multicooker. Add 2 cups water inside, lemongrass and bay leaves.
4. Place the dish with chicken on the trivet and close the lid. Press Manual button and cook on High pressure for 18 minutes. Do the quick release and enjoy!

Nutritional info (per serving): 324 calories; 25 g fat; 1 g total carbs; 2 g protein

Taiwan Inspired Filipino Braised Pork

Cooking Time: 40 minutes

Servings: 4

Ingredients:

- 1 ½ lbs. pork belly (with skin)
- ¼ cup deep fried shallots or minced shallots
- 1 cup cold water
- 8 garlic cloves, minced
- 4 ginger slices
- 3-star anise
- 2 bay leaves
- ½ teaspoon five spice powder
- ¼ teaspoon ground white pepper
- 3 tablespoons soy sauce
- 1 tablespoon dark soy sauce
- 1 tablespoon Shaoxing wine
- 1 tablespoon Chinese black vinegar
- 2 tablespoons brown sugar
- 1 ½ tablespoons unsalted butter

Instructions:

1. Preheat the Multicooker by pressing the Sauté function until is indicates Hot.
2. Add peanut oil.
3. Season pork with salt and place it in the Multicooker. Cook for 3 minutes and set aside.
4. Melt butter in the Multicooker, add brown sugar, and cook for 2 minutes.
5. Sauté shallots, ginger and garlic for 2 minutes.
6. Add wine and water to deglaze, scrape the bottom to ensure nothing sticks.
7. Add star anise, bay leaves, soy sauce, dark soy sauce, black vinegar, five spice powder, ground white pepper and mix well. Turn it off.

8. Chop pork and add to the Multicooker. Close the lid, set valve to Sealed, pressure cook on High pressure for 20 minutes. Naturally release pressure after 10 minutes, open the lid.
9. To thicken the sauce, discard anise and bay leaves, press Sauté mode and cook for 10 minutes.

Nutritional info (per serving): 620 calories; 61 g fat; 5 g total carbs; 11 g protein

Orange Chicken

Cooking Time: 50 minutes

Servings: 4

Ingredients:

- 2 lbs. chicken thighs
- 1 orange, juiced and zested
- 6 garlic cloves, chopped
- 1 tablespoon ginger, crushed
- 1 onion, sliced
- 1 tablespoon peanut oil
- 1 tablespoon Shaoxing wine
- ½ cup unsalted chicken stock
- 2 tablespoons honey
- 2.5 tablespoons cornstarch+ 3 tablespoons cold water
- salt

Marinade:

- 2 tablespoons regular soy sauce
- ½ teaspoon sesame oil
- ¼ teaspoon salt
- ¼ teaspoon sugar

Instructions:

1. Mix marinade ingredients in a small bowl and set aside.
2. Place chicken in a container and pour marinade over it, mix and let it marinate for ½ of an hour.
3. Press the Sauté function on the Multicooker, when it indicates Hot, add peanut oil.
4. Cook onions, ginger and garlic for 2 minutes.
5. Deglaze the pot with wine and scrape the bottom.

6. Add chicken stock, orange juice, orange zest and marinated chicken to the Multicooker. Pressure cook on High pressure for 6 minutes. Naturally release pressure after 10 minutes.
7. Remove chicken and set aside.
8. Press Sauté mode and bring the sauce to a boil, add honey and cornstarch mixture, stir to let the sauce thicken.
9. Serve chicken and drizzle the orange sauce over it.

Nutritional info (per serving): 632 calories; 42 g fat; 22 g total carbs; 39 g protein

Sweet Sour Chicken

Cooking Time: 25 minutes

Servings: 4

Ingredients:

- 1 lbs. chicken breast, cubed
- 12 oz. sweet and sour sauce
- 8 oz. pineapple chunks in can with juice
- 1 cup water
- 1 head broccoli
- tri colored peppers and onions, frozen
- ¼ teaspoon garlic powder
- 1 tablespoon onion flakes
- 1 tablespoon brown sugar
- 2 tablespoons butter, melted

Instructions:

1. Press Sauté mode on the Multicooker and add butter.
2. Add chicken, garlic powder, onion flakes and cook for 5 minutes.
3. Turn it off; add sweet and sour sauce, sugar and water. Press High pressure and cook for 12 minutes. Naturally release pressure for 2 minutes.
4. Add broccoli, pineapples with juice and tri colored peppers. Cook on High pressure for 2 minutes and do a quick release.
5. Serve over rice.

Nutritional info (per serving): 356 calories; 16.8 g fat; 25 g total carbs; 26 g protein

Filipino Asian Pork Shoulder

Cooking Time: 30 minutes

Servings: 4

Ingredients:

- 2 lbs. pork shoulder
- 6 garlic cloves, chopped
- 1 onion, sliced
- 1 tablespoon ginger, chopped
- 2 tablespoons soy sauce
- ½ cup unsalted chicken stock
- 1 tablespoon peanut
- 2 stalks green onions, chopped
- 2.5 tablespoons cornstarch + 3 tablespoons cold water
- Salt, to taste

Instructions:

1. Season pork with salt and pepper.
2. Press Sauté function to preheat the Multicooker, when indicated Hot add peanut oil.
3. Add pork and cook for 5 minutes on each side, set aside.
4. Add onion and garlic to the Multicooker. Cook for 2 minutes.
5. Add chicken stock to deglaze, stir and turn it off.
6. Place pork on a cutting board and cut into thick slices.
7. Add soy sauce and pork to the Multicooker. Close the lid, cook on High pressure for 6 minutes, and then naturally release pressure after 10 minutes.
8. Remove pork slices and set aside.
9. Add green onions and cornstarch mixture. Mix well until it thickens. Turn off heat and add pork back.
10. Serve and enjoy

Nutritional info (per serving): 322 calories; 10 g fat; 31 g total carbs; 24 g protein

About the Author

Melanie Diwata was born and raised in Central Luzon, the Philippines in the late 80s. Her family had a strong agricultural background which exposed her to the varieties of foods revered by the Filipinos. She always watched her mum prepare great Filipino delicacies with great enthusiasm.

Melanie moved to the United States in the late 90s when her Father, John Diwata, got a job in a food processing plant based in Monterey County, California. She was introduced to a porpular multicooker by her friend, Jane Richie, at college. Since then, she has used multicookers and pressure cookers to prepare tasty Filipino meals that have earned her the respect of the community where she lives. Encouraged by the support she got, she decided to write the book titled *"The Filipino Instant Cookbook for Beginners."* Join her as she shares 100 tasty Filipino recipes that can be prepared quickly using porpular multicookers.

Made in the USA
Las Vegas, NV
25 February 2024

86257159R10072